FabJob® Guide to

BECOME A COFFEE HOUSE OWNER

TOM HENNESSY

FABJOB® GUIDE TO BECOME A COFFEE HOUSE OWNER
by Tom Hennessy

ISBN-13: 978-1-894638-60-9

ISBN-10: 1-894638-60-3

Library and Archives Canada Cataloguing in Publication Data

Hennessy, Tom.
    FabJob guide to become a coffee house owner / by Tom Hennessy

Accompanied by a CD-ROM.
Includes bibliographical references.
ISBN 1-894638-60-3

1. Coffeehouses—Management.   2. New business enterprises—Management.   I. Title.
TX911.3.M27H44 2004   647.95'068   C2004-903570-3

Important Disclaimer: Although every effort has been made to ensure this guide is free from errors, this publication is sold with the understanding that the authors, editors, and publisher are not responsible for the results of any action taken on the basis of information in this work, nor for any errors or omissions. The publishers, and the authors and editors, expressly disclaim all and any liability to any person, whether a purchaser of this publication or not, in respect of anything and of the consequences of anything done or omitted to be done by any such person in reliance, whether whole or partial, upon the whole or any part of the contents of this publication. If expert advice is required, services of a competent professional person should be sought.

About the Websites Mentioned in this Guide: Although we aim to provide the information you need within the guide, we have also included a number of websites because readers have told us they appreciate knowing about sources of additional information. (**TIP:** Don't include a period at the end of a web address when you type it into your browser.) Due to the constant development of the Internet, websites can change. Any websites mentioned in this guide are included for the convenience of readers only. We are not responsible for the content of any sites except FabJob.com.

FabJob Inc.
19 Horizon View Court
Calgary, Alberta, Canada T3Z 3M5

FabJob Inc.
4603 NE University Village #224
Seattle, Washington, USA 98105

To order books in bulk phone 403-949-2039
To arrange an author interview phone 403-949-4980

www.FabJob.com
THE DREAM CAREER EXPERTS

About the Author

Tom Hennessy is a 25 year veteran of the restaurant business. He opened his first restaurant when he was 27 and has gone on to own and operate several other concepts including three brewpubs, a large production brewery, a chain of wood oven pizza restaurants, and of course a coffee house.

Tom started writing in high school and college and has written various articles for trade publications and spoken at conventions around the U.S. He has also produced and published a video on building breweries, and is the author of the *Fabjob Guide To Become A Restaurant Owner*. His interest in business focuses on two areas: the quality of the business system, and not spending a fortune setting up your business.

Mr Hennessy currently spends his time working as a ranger for the National Park Service, sailing in Mexico, and helping others start their coffee houses, restaurants, and breweries. He lives with his wife Sandy in Palisade, Colorado. He can be reached at tomhen@mac.com.

Dedication

To Sandy

Contents

1. Introduction

1.1 Owning A Coffee House

In 1984, I was living in Santa Fe, New Mexico, managing a restaurant close to the downtown plaza. I was fortunate enough to live within walking distance of work. This was a real treat, because Santa Fe is an ideal location for walking. There is so much to see: beautiful Pueblo architecture connected by a street layout that was made for donkeys instead of automobiles. It truly is not like most state capitals.

One of my favorite stops on my way to work was a small coffee house on the corner of two well-traveled paths. It was a tiny place, with an espresso machine sitting on a counter and a few pastries displayed behind the glass case. One wall was full of magazines — maybe 75 titles. In between the counter and the magazines was a jumble of marble-top tables for customers to sit at. There was also a spiral stair-case leading to a small loft of about 200 square feet. The loft had comfortable seating, and usually this area was filled with students reading or playing cards or chess. The aroma of coffee perfumed the air; it felt very European to be there, something of a throwback to bo-hemian Paris. You could see that the customers were truly enjoying the atmosphere.

A Coffee House is the Ideal Business

Compared to my restaurant job, this seemed like the ideal business to operate. The idea of a coffee house appeared to be so simple. In my restaurant, I had a staff of about 75; at the coffee house, there were never more than two people working at a time. While my restaurant had a large menu that took hours to prepare, this place had only a few simple items made by a local bakery. I was hooked! My goal was to run a coffee house of my own.

Five years later, I opened my own café in Santa Fe. My business partners were also my best friends. We had already opened three other full-service restaurants, but the café was easier — and a lot more fun. It wasn't even that hard to do. I don't know why I waited so long.

What could be better after an early Sunday morning bike ride than stopping at the local coffee house to meet friends? Who isn't comforted at the idea of a fresh muffin and a steaming cup of aromatic, dark, robust coffee? After going through the process myself, I can tell you that there is only one thing better than going to your local coffee house: owning the local coffee house yourself.

The Origin of Coffee Houses

When you own a coffee house, you become part of a rich culture that dates back to the time of King Solomon. In fact, the first coffee house was opened by Schems and Hekin in Constantinople in 1554. Since that time, the coffee house has come to symbolize a more cultured side of humanity. Historically, it has provided a place for people to gather to discuss politics, music, poetry, romance, or even rebellion. In today's coffee culture, drinking coffee is seen as being social, affluent, and downright hip.

Understanding the Perfect Cup of Coffee

One of the most important requirements of owning a coffee house is loving coffee. That means not only enjoying the flavor or aroma of the drink but also loving the coffee culture as well. I'm not saying coffee has to become a religion, but it's crucial to have an appreciation of the coffee roaster's craft.

Familiarize yourself with the roasting process. Get to know the character of the bean and how to ensure the perfect roast. Understand all the nuances of grinding and brewing a perfect cup of coffee. And finally, teach your staff how to do all of these things consistently too.

1.2 What a Coffee House Owner Does

A coffee house owner should be fully educated in all the nuances of coffee, from coffee house lingo to production to brewing to serving. Therefore, let's go over some of these basics before we get into the nuts and bolts of the coffee house business.

1.2.1 Coffee House Lingo

All businesses develop their own language, but I don't think any is as colorful as the coffee business. Remember that scene in the movie *L.A. Story* where a group of friends are sitting around a table in a trendy restaurant, and the waiter asks if anyone would like to have coffee after their meal? That begins a round of ordering every type of coffee drink imaginable — a very funny scene when "coffee house hip" culture was only thriving in a few places in North America.

What was hip then is the norm now. So to get familiar with the many ways your customers may be ordering coffee from you, it is best to go over the different types of coffee names, as well as other business lingo that is used in restaurants and coffee houses. It is a language all by itself, one that can be fun to learn.

86	To get rid of, as in "86 the cinnamon."
Americano	Espresso with hot water added to dilute it. Similar to drip coffee, except it is made to order with your espresso machine.
Barista	The person who operates the espresso machine, much like a bartender.
Breve	Espresso with half-and-half.

Café Au Lait	Drip coffee with hot or boiled milk poured into a cup at the same time.
Café Con Leche	Espresso with enough steamed milk to fill a regular-sized cup.
Café Con Panna	A demitasse (small cup) of espresso with a dollop of whipped cream.
Café Corretto	Espresso with cognac or some other spirit added.
Café Crème	A shot of espresso with an ounce of heavy cream.
Café Freddo	Espresso served in a chilled glass, mostly over ice.
Café Latte	The most popular coffee drink. A shot of espresso with steamed milk, topped with foamed milk.
Café Macchiato	A shot of espresso with a teaspoon or two of foamed milk. "Macchiato" means marked, so you are marking the espresso with a touch of foamed milk.
Café Medici	A double espresso with chocolate and a touch of whipped cream. Usually, this is made with chocolate syrup, but occasionally a barista may use a small chunk of real chocolate in the bottom of the cup, then brew the espresso on top. It will melt some of the chocolate – but not all of it – leaving a nice chocolate treat at the bottom.
Café Mocha	A café latte with chocolate added. It can just have the foamed milk on top, or have whipped cream with chocolate sprinkled as a finish.

Café Ristretto	A short shot of espresso, using the same amount of coffee as a regular shot. This just means that you don't run the espresso machine as long, so there is less liquid. The result is a stronger, more concentrated coffee.
Cake in a Cup	A double shot of espresso with double cream and double sugar.
Cappuccino	A shot of espresso with foamed milk spooned on top.
Crema	The caramel-colored foam that comes to the surface of the espresso — much like the head on a beer, only slightly thinner. The crema is vital to a good espresso. It is made up of the solubles that pass through during the brewing process.
Demitasse	A small espresso cup. It should be only large enough for a single espresso. This attractive cup is for the straight espresso with nothing else added.
Doppio	This is just the Italian way to order a double. It sounds better than saying "double."
Drip	Regular coffee.
Dry	With just foam and no steamed milk.
Espresso	The coffee brewed from an espresso machine. Hot water is pressed through the coffee by way of a pump or a piston, as compared to a drip machine, which uses gravity.
Frappuccino	A Starbucks creation. Basically a chilled cappuccino that is sweetened and has other flavor ingredients. The recipe is owned by Starbucks.

Grande	A 16-ounce cup.
Granita	A latte with frozen milk.
Half-Caff	Any coffee drink made half with caffeinated coffee and half with decaf.
Harmless	A cool way to say you want your drink as a decaf.
Mochaccino	Like a café mocha except on a cappuccino instead of a latte.
Nico	A breve with orange syrup and cinnamon.
On a Leash	Ordered to go with handles (referring to the cup).
Quad	Four shots, or a "double double."
Rice Dream Latte	A latte made with rice dream — a non-dairy milk replacement.
Short	An 8-ounce cup.
Shot	A single dose of espresso.
Shot in the Dark	Drip coffee with a single shot of espresso in it.
Single	Same as a shot.
Skinny	A latte or cappuccino made with nonfat milk instead of regular milk.
Skinny Harmless	Nonfat, decaf. But I like the other name for it: "Why Bother?"
Soy Latte	A latte made with soy milk instead of regular milk.

Tall	A 12-ounce cup.
Triple	Three shots.
Two-Top	A table for two. (You'll also encounter "three-top," "four-top," etc.)
Unleaded	Another good way of saying "decaf."
Venti	A 20-ounce cup.
Wet	Add steamed milk with no foam.
Whipless	No whipped cream.
With Legs	A cup with handles.
With Room	Leaving space at the top so the customer can add cream.

You may decide to use all of these terms or just some of them, or you may learn new ones. In any case, they can be a lot of fun if you let your customers in on the lingo. Try printing a list of terms and putting them on a table-tent (a printed card that is placed on the tables). This way, your customers can learn the lingo while sipping their "tall skinny half-caff."

1.2.2 Coffee Basics

Coffee comes from bean-shaped seeds found inside the cherrylike fruits of coffee trees and shrubs. While the coffee plant originated in Africa, it eventually found its way to other continents as well. There are many types of coffee plants, but we only need to concentrate on two types: Arabica and Robusta.

Robusta coffee is grown at lower elevations and is used in cheaper blends and instant coffees. When you buy coffee in a can, it is usually Robusta. It has more caffeine than its Arabica cousin. The beans have a more rounded shape to them, which makes them easy to recognize.

Arabica coffee is grown at higher elevations and has more of an oval-shaped bean. These beans are of a higher quality and represent the majority of the beans grown in the world. As the owner of a quality coffee house, you will be buying this type of bean.

Processing

A single coffee tree will produce approximately one pound of coffee — around 2,000 beans. Each cherry is handpicked and then fed into a machine to separate the cherry meat from the seeds, or beans. The beans are held long enough to ferment, which breaks down their coating and raises their acidity.

Afterwards, the beans are dried, either in the sun on concrete slabs or in drum-style dryers. When the beans have dried sufficiently, a protective husk needs to be removed. This is accomplished by milling the beans, which gently crushes them, removing this protective skin. Finally, the beans are sorted, graded, and allowed to dry before shipping to the roaster.

Roasting

Once the person doing the roasting receives the beans, he or she will determine the type of roast that is best for that particular variety. While there are general guidelines, much depends on the roaster's preferences and tastes.

The actual roasting machine is a rotating drum with a heat source underneath it. Once the desired temperature is reached inside the machine, the beans are added and the drum constantly turns until the target roast is achieved. This process is timed down to the exact second. Meanwhile, the roaster pulls samples to visually inspect the beans.

During the roasting process, heat breaks down the cellular structure of the beans, which allows the aromatic oils and other flavor compounds to escape. How long and dark the beans are roasted dictates the character of the flavors the beans will yield. Different characteristics can also be achieved by blending various types of beans from different geographic locations and at different roasts to achieve a coffee that is truly a signature flavor.

TIP: Working at a Starbucks or at some other large coffee house is the best way to get hands-on experience. Even if you only work one day a week, you will still get great ideas to carry over to your own coffee house.

1.3 Inside This Guide

The *FabJob Guide to Become a Coffee House Owner* is a step-by-step guide that show you how to open your own coffee house and how to keep it going.

Chapter 2 will get you thinking about what kind of coffee house you want to own. We'll cover different approaches to starting this type of business and show you how to tackle writing a business plan. You'll also learn about hiring a lawyer and an accountant and tapping into funding sources.

In Chapter 3, we'll take you through the process of finding the right location for your coffee house and making sure that the space you choose is inviting. You'll also learn how to hire the right contractor and meet coding and inspection requirements. Buying the right supplies and equipment and teaming up with quality food distributors are also important, and we'll tell you what you need to know.

Chapter 4 focuses on how to run your coffee house. Here, we'll delve into the details of the business, covering everything from how to roast your own beans to how to choose the best lighting, from planning a tempting menu to getting to know your customers. You'll also get detailed information about creating the right atmosphere for your shop.

Chapter 5 covers the big moment: opening your coffee house. In this chapter, you'll find out how to get bodies through the door — and keep them there.

Chapter 6 will fill you in on the daily operations of managing your coffee house. This includes hiring staff, training employees, keeping the books, and lots of other information crucial to helping you maintain a well-run business.

Chapter 7 takes you through everything you'll need to keep your business financially viable, from keeping a budget to tracking sales. We'll also give you tips on building wealth and paying off debt, vital skills for any successful business owner to have a handle on.

Finally, the list of resources at the end of the book lists valuable websites, books, and trade magazines that can help you gain even more knowledge about this rewarding career.

The purpose of owning a coffee house is to be able to do something interesting for a living. The goal is to build a business that will last a long time. You may want to keep it simple and still know all of your customers by their first names, or you may want to expand. Either way, if you apply what you learn in this guide, you'll become a successful coffee house owner in no time.

As of 2006, that coffee house in Santa Fe is still in business. So don't let people tell you that owning a coffee house is too risky. Failing to live your dreams is the only real risk in life.

2. Starting Your Own Coffee House

Maybe you've always dreamed of owning a coffee house. Maybe you live in a community where there aren't any coffee houses, and you think there should be one. Maybe there aren't any good places for people to gather in your community, and you believe that a coffee house could fill this need. All of these are good reasons to start your own coffee house.

Or perhaps you've noticed a local coffee house for sale. You like the work it does, and it's in a location that you know is a good one. You could buy it and operate it, taking advantage of its already established reputation and customer base.

Deciding which route is right for you is an important decision. An established shop will cost more than starting from scratch, but it will also come with customers, inventory, and reputation — which means that it will be likely to continue with its pre-established success. A new shop typically costs less to start up, and you can tailor it specifically to your own vision. But you will need to spend some money on advertising, gaining clientele, and making a reputation for your business—and new businesses have a higher risk of failure. Still, starting your own coffee house can be an extremely rewarding investment.

2.1 Options for Starting a Coffee House

2.1.1 Buying an Established Shop

As already mentioned, one option for getting into the coffee house business is to buy an existing shop and make it your own. Sam Jones, owner of 2 Percent Jazz Espresso (**www.2percentjazz.com**) in Victoria, British Columbia, opened his coffee house in 1997. Sam chose to buy an existing restaurant because of the simplicity of doing a remodel instead of starting from scratch.

When you assume ownership of an existing coffee house, you'll still need a business plan, financing, a lawyer, and an accountant, but many of the other decisions – like what to call the shop and where to locate it – will already have been made. In addition, depending on the sale, you may acquire existing equipment, furniture, supplies, and clientele. However, you also may have to assume any liabilities that come with the shop, such as any outstanding payments it may owe to its suppliers.

If you make what's called a stock purchase, it means you are buying everything, from inventory to liabilities. You will be responsible for any debts the shop has incurred. If you make what's called an asset purchase, you will only be buying the material part of the shop, and the previous owner will be responsible for any outstanding financial matters.

You can expect to pay anywhere from $30,000 to more than $200,000 for an existing coffee house. I've seen shops for as much as $400,000, but the average price seems to be around $150,000. This usually includes all supplies and equipment and often means taking over an existing lease or rental agreement for the location. Pricing for restaurants is based on the cost of the store's supplies and on a percentage of its total annual sales.

As a business broker, I learned that most deals aren't cash purchases but rather are owner financed, which means that the owner doesn't sell the business to a buyer for cash or with bank financing, like in most real estate deals. Instead, they sell their business for a down payment and then take the rest of the sales price over a period of time, with interest. Let me give you an example.

Let's assume that you've found an ideal restaurant for sale that you believe would make a perfect coffee house. The owner wants $100,000. As part of your negotiations, you state that you will pay full price if the owner will finance the outstanding balance after your down payment.

So the deal would look like this: At closing, you would give the owner a check for $20,000 and sign a contract saying that you will pay the rest of the purchase price ($80,000) over a period of five years, including interest, in monthly installments. The owner gets the full asking price, steady income over the next five years, and interest on the $80,000. You get a $100,000 restaurant plus a fast start on building your coffee house for just $20,000 out of pocket — without having to go to the bank.

You don't need to have any experience in the restaurant industry to buy a coffee house and begin operating it, but you do need to have the energy to devote yourself to learning as you go along. You also need to stick with it. Plan on it taking from two to five years to earn back your purchase price.

If you decide this is the route you want to take, you should begin by looking for coffee houses for sale in your area. Or, if you're feeling adventurous, maybe even look outside your immediate area. Of course, you'll need to make sure you can support yourself, afford the move, pay for your new business expenses, and maintain good credit.

If there is already something in the location you want, it's worth simply asking the owner if he will sell the business. I was a business broker for a while, concentrating on restaurants, and I found that almost every business I called was interested in selling. Who isn't, if the price is right?

You can also ask local owners if they know of any other coffee house owners who are considering retirement. Look in your local newspaper, ask at the Chamber of Commerce, or read local business publications.

Shops for Sale

Believe it or not, eBay has coffee houses for sale. On the "search" page, type "coffee" as your search word, and choose "Real Estate" in the Category drop-down menu.

There are several other websites that list restaurants and coffee houses for sale as well. Use words like "coffee," "café," and "espresso" when entering keywords into a website's search engine. Some of these sites include:

- *BizBuySell*
  www.bizbuysell.com

- *BusinessNation*
  www.businessnation.com/Businesses_for_Sale/ Food-Restaurant/

- *BusinessForSale.com*
  www.businessesforsale.com

- *BizQuest*
  www.bizquest.com

- *BizBen.com*
  (Only for California, but it's still quite a list!)
  www.bizben.com/index.php

TIP: Beware websites that require you to pay a fee to see listings. Real estate agents make their money on sales, and not on people browsing.

While I chose these websites because they listed several coffee houses and don't require a paid membership to browse the postings, if you want to check out more business-for-sale websites, search in Google or another search engine for "business for sale," in quotes.

2.1.2 Franchising

If you are eager to start your open your own coffee house but are concerned about how much work is involved in getting everything set up, you may want to consider franchising.

What is Franchising?

Franchising happens when an established company allows someone to run a local business using its company name, logo, products, services, marketing, and business systems. The original company is known as the "franchisor" and the company that is granted the right to run its business is known as the "franchisee."

You have probably bought products and services from many franchisees. For example, if you have ever sat down to a cup of coffee from Dunkin' Donuts, Barnie's Coffee & Tea Co, or even a McDonald's, you were buying from a franchise. (And, in case you're wondering, Starbucks is not a franchise.)

Pros and Cons of Franchising

People who choose to franchise rather than start their own business from scratch often do so because they want to minimize their risk. They see the franchise as a proven business that already has name recognition among the public. By working with an established system, franchisees hope to avoid costly mistakes and make a profit more quickly.

Franchises are also good for people who want support. Franchisors typically provide training to help franchisees start, market, and run their new business. The franchisee may receive assistance with everything from obtaining supplies to setting up record-keeping systems. Many franchisors are continuously working to develop better systems and products, and franchisees can take advantage of those developments. Some provide comprehensive training and "secrets" of making the perfect cup of coffee.

It is important to keep in mind that a franchisee does not own any of the company's trademarks or business systems. Also, a franchisee must run her business according to the terms of her agreement with the franchisor. For example, the franchisee may not be permitted to offer a sales promotion or use a supplier that has not been authorized by the franchisor.

While some people appreciate having such guidelines to follow, if you are an independent person who enjoys taking risks and being spontaneous, you might find owning a franchise to be too restrictive.

Since someone else is ultimately "in charge," you may be wondering how having a franchise is different from being an employee. In fact, there are significant differences. You have more freedom than an employee would (you might choose your own working hours, for example). And you could ultimately earn a lot more money than an employee.

On the other hand, franchisees must pay thousands of dollars up front for the opportunity to work with the business, and there is the possibility that the franchise will not be financially successful. Many websites on the topic of franchising claim more than a 90 percent long-term success rate for franchisees. However, the Business Link website cites a study reported in the *Wall Street Journal* that found a 35 percent failure rate for franchises. Your own success will depend on a variety of factors, including your geographical location and the particular franchise you become involved with.

> **TIP:** If you are considering franchising, do your homework and gather all the information you need to make an informed decision. What you receive for your investment varies from franchise to franchise, so make sure you know exactly what you will be buying and make sure that any claims are substantiated. Before signing a contract, it is also wise to consult with people you trust, such as your accountant or attorney, to give you unbiased and sound advice.

Coffee House Franchises

There are numerous coffee house franchises. Some offer pastries or other restaurant style treats in addition to coffee, and some are small kiosks that sell only coffee and tea drinks. You can find more information about the franchises listed below by doing a search at the International Franchise Association website (**www.franchise.org**).

Costs

Estimated start-up costs for a coffee house franchise range from $25,000 to $400,000. The initial investment typically includes two components: the payment of a franchise fee and other start-up costs

Entrepreneur Magazine describes a franchise fee as a one-time charge paid to the franchisor "for the privilege of using the business concept, attending their training program, and learning the entire business." Other start-up costs may include equipment, building and leasing expenses, food supplies (including coffee beans), and other must-haves, like paper goods and dishes for customers. For excellent advice on franchises, visit the magazine's website at **www.entrepreneur.com/ Franchise_Zone**.

A franchise fee for a coffee house tends to be around $25,000, with much of the investment money going to other business needs as mentioned above.

There are a variety of factors involved in determining the initial investment, including:

- The geographic area you will be working in

- The nature of your business (will you have a kiosk or a drive-thru, or will you serve extras, like pastries, soups, and sandwiches?)

- The particular company you franchise with

In addition to your initial investment, you can expect to pay the franchisor ongoing royalties. These royalties typically range from seven percent to 11 percent of your sales; the exact amount will depend on the company you franchise with.

Franchisors

The companies listed here are provided only for your information. They are not recommendations. Only you can decide which franchise, if any, will be best for you.

- *Bad Ass Coffee Co.*
  www.badasscoffee.com

- *Barnie's Coffee & Tea Co.*
  www.barniescoffee.com/ecomm/Home.jsp

- *Beaner's Gourmet Coffee*
  www.beaners.com

- *Big Apple Bagels*
  www.babcorp.com

- *Café Ala Carte*
  www.cafealacarte.com

- *Capri Coffee Break*
  www.capricoffee.com

- *Chock full o' Nuts*
  www.chockfullonuts.com/Cafe

- *The Coffee Beanery*
  www.coffeebeanery.com

- *Crescent City Beignets*
  www.crescentcitybeignets.com

- *Dunkin' Donuts*
  www.dunkin-baskin-togos.com/html/home.asp

- *Dunn Bros Coffee*
  http://www.dunnbros.com

- *Gloria Jean's Gourmet Coffees Franchising Corp.*
  www.gloriajeans.com

- *Gourmet Cup*
  www.shefield.com/gourmetcup

- *Hawaii's Java Kai*
  www.javakai.com

- *It's A Grind*
  www.itsagrind.com

- *Jo to Go — The Drive Thru Espresso Bar*
  www.jotogo.com

- *Jumpin' Juice & Java*
  www.jumpinjuiceandjava.com/start.htm

- *LaMar's Donuts*
  www.lamars.com

- *Maui Wowi*
  www.mauiwowi.com/franchising

- *Mocha Delites Inc.*
  www.mochadelites.com/home.html

- *Nestle Toll House — Café by Chip*
  www.nestlecafe.com/home

- *PJ's Coffee & Tea Co.*
  www.pjscoffee.com/customer/index.php

- *The Second Cup Ltd.*
  www.secondcup.com

- *Seekers Coffee House*
  www.seekerscoffeehouse.com

- *Shefield Gourmet*
  www.shefieldgourmet.com

- *Tim Hortons*
  www.timhortons.com

- *Tropical Smoothie Café*
  www.tropicalsmoothie.com

- *Van Houtte Inc.*
  www.vanhoutte.com

You can also get free personalized help online by going to **www.Franchise-Consultation.com**.

2.1.3 Opening a New Coffee House

Of course, you can always start from scratch and open a brand new coffee house. That way, you can have complete control over every step of the process and make sure that your shop is everything you want it to be.

2.2 Getting Started

This section will show you how to start your own business, using a 50-seat coffee house as an example. The coffee house will serve a limited menu of pastries, soups, salads, and sandwiches. It will not roast its own coffee but rather will purchase its beans wholesale. Depending on how large a shop you want to open, you can add or subtract from this information to suit your own plans or interests.

2.2.1 Creating a Business Plan

Don't let a business plan scare you. There seems to be a lot of mystery surrounding the creation of a business plan, when in fact it's really quite simple. The purpose of this document is twofold. First, it's intended to help you think through the whole business and create a map for where you want to go with it. Second, it helps to show sources of possible financial backing that you have thought your business through and that it is viable.

Bill and Cheryl Mehaffey decided to quit their jobs in the medical research field. They moved from Wisconsin to Colorado and opened their own coffee house and roastery in the Colorado mountains. When they first started, they were not sure where to begin. Fortunately, they found a class being offered by the Small Business Administration at their local community college on how to write a business plan. This was their first step in the creation of Bongo Billy's Café, which opened in Buena Vista, Colorado, in 1994.

Bongo Billy's (**www.bongobillys.com**) has become famous in Colorado for the quality of its coffee and the professionalism of its operation. Bill is still appreciative of the lessons he learned at those first classes. "It was an important first step," he says. "It made us consider all the details we needed to think through in order to get started." Writing a business plan is the starting point in this adventure.

Following are descriptions of the essential parts of a business plan. If you want to see what a business plan looks like, you can find an online guide to writing a business plan at the Small Business Administration website. Check it out at **www.sba.gov/starting/indexbusplans.html**.

Executive Summary

This first section is a quick overview of your coffee house that really doesn't need to be more than four or five pages long. Include a short introduction followed by subsections with headings such as:

Management

List any members of your management team and their work experience. If your "team" consists of just you, elaborate as much as you can. Leave the reader with a sense that there will be a competent management team in place.

Concept

Go through the details of the concept. Try to paint a picture of what your coffee house will look like, what it will serve, and what kind of people you believe will be your customers. (You will have a better idea of where you are going with this by the time you finish reading this guide.)

Growth Potential

Include some statistics about the growth of the coffee business and how you feel that you are positioned in this market to grow your own business. A good source of information for writing this section is a trade magazine called *The Specialty Coffee Retailer*, which you can read online at **www.specialty-coffee.com**.

Competition

List who you feel your competition would be in your market. This could include other coffee houses, coffee carts, coffee kiosks in grocery stores, or restaurants that serve quality coffee.

Financial Requirements

This section covers how much it will cost you to get into business. Before you start your coffee house, it is important to have a good idea of how much you are going to spend.

Cash Flow

I like to add a section that shows a monthly projection of cash coming in and cash going out. This information will give you a good idea of how much you need to sell in order to survive and prosper.

With this first section, you don't need to get too detailed with your business descriptions. The reader is just getting a taste of what you plan to do. In the following sections, you will elaborate on all of this.

Organizational Plan

This section discusses the inner workings of your coffee house. Basically, you want the person reading it to know in more detail how you will set up your business. Here are some ideas of what to include.

Start with a more detailed description of the business, including the theme. You can give some examples of existing coffee houses you have seen or know about. It is okay to include copies of articles about similar businesses with pictures that will give the reader an idea of the "look" of the place.

Identify the legal structure of your business, such as whether it is a corporation or a partnership. The person reading this will want to know how the business will be structured.

Explain how your bookkeeping system will operate. In other words, identify who your accountant will be and state that the accountant will be processing a monthly profit and loss report. (See section 7.1.1 for more information on this.) Potential investors will want a copy of this every month, and it is a good idea to let them know from the start that you will have this information available.

Financial Section

Now come the guts of the whole thing: the financial part. First, put together a spreadsheet that shows how much you believe the whole project will cost. This should include the cost of renovating the space; of the equipment; of the capital you'll need in order to buy your initial inventories; of organizational costs like legal and accounting; plus licensing fees, marketing costs, the price of training employees, and a cushion of cash to get you started. The total amount will be what it costs you to get into business.

Use the sample spreadsheet on the next few pages to help you with your own numbers. These are typical cost figures for a 50-seat coffee house. In this case, an existing restaurant was obtained that needed only a slight remodeling.

Estimated Costs For 50-Seat Coffee House

Projected Total Cost: $96,711

Coffee House Setup

Item	Budget	Item	Budget
Legal	$ 500	Dues	$ 100
Accounting	500	Food Inventory	2,500
Architect	1,500	Beverage Inventory	1,500
Rent Deposits	3,000	Supplies Inventory	1,500
License Fees	500	Training Costs	8,000
Insurance Deposit	100	Working Capital	10,000

Total Setup Costs **$29,700**

Construction

Item	Budget	Item	Budge
Plumbing	$ 5,000	Electrical	$ 5,000
Framing and Cabinetry	15,000	Miscellaneous	4,000

Total Construction Costs **$29,000**

Equipment

Item	Budget	Item	Budget
Espresso Machine	$ 2,640	Pre-rinse	$ 205
Water Filter	155	Dishwasher *(leased)*	0
2 Espresso Grinders	1,230	30 Qt. Mixer	3,625
Coffee Brewer	1,160	One-Door Freezer	1,290
Ice Bin	365	Walk-in Cooler	2,295
Reach-in Cooler	1,420	Ice Machine	1,185
Sandwich Prep Table	1,670	Microwave Oven	530
Stove w/ Oven	2,325	Metro Shelves	528
Prep Tables	530	Bus Cart	120
Dish Tables	810	Grease Trap	610
Hood and Make-Up Air	795	Soda Dispenser	0
Fire Suppression System	1,740	*(provided by soda purveyor)*	
Kitchen Aid Mixer	420	Food Processor	695
Three-Compartment Sink	750	Power Mixer	495
Mop Sink	180		

Total Equipment Costs **$27,768**

Furniture and Fixtures

Item	Budget	Item	Budget
Tables	$ 940	Artwork	$ 1,000
Table Bases	250	Booster Chairs	36
Portable Coffee Bar	655	High Chairs	88
Chairs and Bar Stools	2,540		

Total Furniture and Fixtures Cost   **$ 5,509**

Small Wares

Item	Budget	Item	Budget
4 Vacuum Pots	$ 216	6-oz. Ladle	$ 4
4 Sheet Pans	20	1-oz. Ladle	2
6 Pie Pans	31	Stock Pot	87
4 Muffin Pans	172	Brazier	120
2 Chef Knives	202	Saucepans	55
Sharpening Steel	24	Sauté Pan	44
2 Chef Spoons	6	Colander	61
Perforated Chef Spoon	62	4 Hotel Pans	52
China Cap Strainer	34	Flatware Holders	17
12 Insert Pans	163	All-Purpose Shelf	59
6 Bus Tubs	86	Slim Trash Can	32
4 Spring Form Pans	38	Conversion Dolly	29
Can Opener	80	Large Trash Can	32
Ice Scoop	560	Mop Bucket	40
Flour Scoop	760	Large Plates	350
2 Flour Bins	144	Small Plates	173
Ounce Scale	53	36 Bowls	219
Pound Scale	57	36 Espresso Cups	166
Hand-Held Thermometer	7	36 Espresso Saucers	100
4 Metal Tongs	11	36 Cappuccino, Latte Cups	330
4 Large Stainless Bowls	56	36 Cappuc., Latte Saucers	110
Wire Whisk	7	24 Creamers	100
4 Large Rubber Spatulas	7	12 Sugar Caddies	52
Cake/Pie Marker	5	12 Tea Pots	170
6 Dishwasher Racks	110	72 Pint Glasses	111
5 Rubber Mats	275	36 Small Glasses	43
Salt and Pepper Shakers	18	72 Forks	76
3 White Cutting Boards	63	72 Teaspoons	60
Pastry Bag	4	36 Soup Spoons	38
Pastry Tips	13	72 Ice Tea Spoons	80
2 Measuring Cups	16	72 Knives	150
Measuring Spoons	6	Timer	12

Total Small Wares Cost   **$ 4,734**

Sample Monthly Cash Flow Sheet

Income

Food	$ 13,320
Beverage	21,600
Merchandise	1,080
Total Sales	**36,000**

Cost of Sales

Food	3,330
Beverage	5,400
Merchandise	756
Total Cost of Sales	**9,486**

Gross Profit $ 26,514

Controllable Expense

Labor	$ 10,000
Supplies	1,200
Replacement Expense	150
Advertising	720
Maintenance and Repairs	300
Music	30
Office Expense	50
Payroll Taxes	1,200
Telephone	175
Utilities	600
Total Controllable Expense	**14,425**

Non-Controllable Expense

Bonus Expense	$ 300
Credit Card Fees	206
Insurance	350
Loans ($80,000 @ 7% for 5 years)	5,698
Accounting	100
License Expense	25
Rent	2,000
Professional Services	25
Total Non-Controllable Expense	**8,704**

Net Cash Flow $ 3,385

Next, you will create a cash flow sheet that is a snapshot of a one-month period. This will start with projected sales, followed by cost of sales (the raw costs of what you are selling), then gross profit (sales minus cost of sales equals gross profit). After gross profit, list your labor and labor taxes, followed by all the other expenses you will have. This will give you a reasonable guess of how much you will need in sales to survive in business.

Use the sample on the previous page as a template for your one-month cash flow. To make this sheet, I used an example of a 50-seat coffee house that cost $100,000 with $20,000 of your own money and $80,000 borrowed from a bank, friends, or investors. For the labor figure, I assumed the coffee house to be owner operated and that it will be open from 6:00 a.m. until 7:00 p.m.

As you will see, the annual projection is essentially in the same format as the one-month cash flow, except that it has twelve columns, one for each month. The same figures should be used, but try to account for busy times and slow times of the year based on your personal knowledge of the town. Also, you can make adjustments for certain things such as yearly fees or taxes due. Your local Chamber of Commerce can help you determine this.

Extend your annual cash flow sheet out over the next five years. It sounds like a lot of work, but once you have the initial month-to-month cash flow sheet made, the rest just involves taking those figures and multiplying them.

Your Management Plan

Include a section that states your management plan. This is a sheet that explains how you will manage the coffee house. Do you plan to manage it by yourself, or will you hire other managers to watch the shop when you are not there? Much of this will depend on your hours of operation, but it is important to address these issues on paper.

Another good inclusion to the management plan would be a weekly work schedule outlining who will be managing what shifts. Include a résumé for each manager — even one for yourself.

Don't worry if you haven't actually hired someone yet. Even if you have only initially interviewed potential managers, you can ask them if you may include their résumés in the business plan. Potential funding sources like to see that you have thought out who will actually be working in your coffee house.

Your Marketing Plan

You need to include a section on demographics, or why you think your business will succeed in your town. One of the best places to obtain information on demographics is from your local Chamber of Commerce. They have information about the town in general and can provide specific data about income levels, education, and other businesses that are located in your town. They may even have color-coded maps to help you easily locate areas that meet your specific demographic needs.

Another source of information might be your local newspaper or radio station. These businesses keep demographic information for advertising purposes and will also be interested in what you are doing anyway and may even keep an eye on your progress. New coffee houses or restaurants are always good material for newspapers or radio stations to report on. So don't be shy in contacting them to let them know what you are up to.

A Sample Menu

In the back section of your business plan, it's a good idea to include a sample menu for your coffee house. That way, potential investors can see what will be served, and the menu also helps the reader get a feel for what the coffee house will be like. (See section 4.2.1 for tips on creating menus.)

2.2.2 Forming a Company

If you are going to be in business, you must first decide what form of business the government will recognize you as. This will involve meeting with your lawyer and accountant (see section 2.2.3 for more information about finding lawyers and accountants). For now, however, there are essentially four types of companies you can form.

Corporation

A corporation appears impressive. This is when you get to put those three letters – Inc. – after your business name. There is a lot to be said for choosing to become a corporation, which basically means that you are creating an entity unto itself.

The reasons for doing this are all about liability. As a corporation, Mike's House of Big Java, Inc. owns the business, instead of Mike owning it himself. Mike just owns the stock in the corporation. This way, if someone decides to sue Mike's House of Big Java, they are suing the company, not the owner. The lawsuit does not "pass through" the corporation to Mike, consequently taking everything he owns. By protecting Mike from being sued, he is able to avoid bankruptcy if his company cannot pay its settlement costs.

Of course, it is not as simple as this. Your lawyer can explain everything in detail and can also explain the difference between a "C" corporation, which does not allow any pass-through profits or losses onto your personal taxes, and an "S" corporation, which does.

Corporations in Canada offer the same liability protections as those in the U.S. If your business is Canadian controlled, you can also get a better tax rate on your first $200,000 of income.

Sole Proprietorship

If you want to run the business yourself without incorporating, your business will be known as a "sole proprietorship." This is the least expensive way to start a business. It is also the easiest because it requires less paperwork and you can report your business income on your personal tax return. One drawback to this type of business is that you are personally liable for any debts of the business.

Partnership

If you choose a partnership, you will want to make some agreements with your partner that will cover essential details. These details could include compensation, raising capital, admission of new partners, hours expected to work, and, most importantly, how one of you can leave the partnership.

All of your profits and losses are passed through to your personal tax reporting. So if the company loses money, you can show the losses against any income you personally have. Conversely, any profits the company has will pass through to you and be taxed at your tax bracket. Also, all the company's liability can pass through to you as well. If someone slips and falls in your coffee house and decides to sue, they will be suing you personally. Don't let this scare you though; that's why you are insured. (See section 2.2.4 to find out about insurance.)

Limited Liability Company (LLC)

If you are based in the United States, you can form another kind of business called a Limited Liability Company (LLC). This is not a corporation, but it offers some of the same liability protection. An LLC also has the pass-through tax benefits of a sole proprietorship or partnership. This allows you to pass through the profits or losses to your own tax liability, which may save you money.

2.2.3 Hiring a Lawyer and an Accountant

You will almost definitely need to hire a lawyer and an accountant to help you understand all of this. Here is some of what you need to know about hiring these individuals.

Your Lawyer

Your lawyer should be a corporate attorney, not one who defends or sues. This person will know how best to set up your business to protect you from litigation. For example, if a customer slips and falls in your coffee house, the way your business is set up may help protect you from being named personally in any lawsuit that may result from an injury.

A lawyer will also know how to work with accountants so that your business structure makes the most legal and financial sense. They will not only recommend what type of business structure to use but will also show you how to include special provisions in your organization, such as buy-sell agreements between you and your partners.

An attorney will also show you how to set up insurance in case you die or are disabled. The insurance would fund the company to buy out your heirs or pay a salary for someone to take your place if you are unable to work. It can get pretty complicated, which is why you need a good lawyer.

Your Accountant

When you are looking for an accountant, try to find one who has some experience in the restaurant business. This means that they should have other clients who own restaurants. You don't want to be this person's test case, as all businesses are different. Ask if they have any other restaurant clients.

There are certain services you will need from your accountant. Besides doing your year-end and quarterly taxes, they should also provide you with a monthly profit and loss statement, or P&L. (We'll go over this more in depth later.) With your monthly P&L, your accountant will also give you a schedule of what taxes need to be paid and when. You can do many of these things yourself, depending on your comfort level, but with some things, it is better to pay the experts while you concentrate on your business.

Some accountants also process payrolls. Again, this is something I suggest you let the experts do. Employees don't like it when their paychecks are incorrect. If the accountant doesn't perform this, there are plenty of payroll companies that do. Just look in your telephone book, or ask another local small business for a recommendation. Payroll-processing companies usually only charge around a dollar per pay-check and can produce nifty payroll reports to boot.

Think of it this way: When setting up your company, you are going into competition with other businesses. It only makes sense to assemble the best team you can to help you succeed. There are plenty of places where you can save money, but good legal and accounting represen-tation is not the area to scrimp on. If you are seriously going to start this coffee house, you want a solid foundation on which to build your company.

2.2.4 Insurance

Choosing the right kind of insurance for your business is critical. You'll need to insure your location, your business contents, and even your-self. It's a complicated matter that your local insurance agency can and should help you with. To find a reputable insurance company, ask other small business owners in your area for recommendations. Chances are they will be willing to help, as strong new businesses can often attract people to spend money at surrounding shops. (Just be sure not to ask any direct competitors!)

Insurances to ask an insurance agent about include:

- Liability insurance. Laws regarding liability change all the time, so be sure you get the latest information about them. Nearly all businesses require liability insurance because there are so many types of liability.

- Property insurance. This will cover your actual shop. If you rent space, the owner of the building normally would pay for insur-ance on the property.

- Disability insurance. If you become sick or otherwise disabled for an extended period of time, your business could be in jeop-ardy. Disability insurance would provide at least a portion of your income while you're not able to work.

- Business interruption insurance. In the event that your property or equipment is damaged or destroyed, this type of insurance covers ongoing expenses such as rent or taxes until your business gets up and running again.

TIP: Make sure you have the insurance you need, but don't let a salesperson talk you into buying all kinds of extra riders and policies. Develop a good understanding of what's required, and stand firm when a salesperson tries to talk you into buying more than that.

An article titled "Determining Your Insurance Needs" has a good explanation of insurance options for small businesses in the United States. You can read the article at **http://sba.gov/test/wbc/docs/finance/insure_needs.html**.

The Insurance Bureau of Canada has information that explains what kinds of insurance you need in Canada and why. Their website is located at **www.ibc.ca/bc.asp**.

2.2.5 Funding Sources

Things are getting ready to roll, and now it's time to pay for it. There are many different streams to dip your coffee house ladle into. When it comes to financing a business, most people think of one source – a bank – when in reality, your funding is probably going to come from a patchwork of different places:

- Your own resources

- Banks

- Leasing companies (for equipment)

- Trades

- Investors

- Family and friends

- Your creativity

Your Own Resources

The starting point will be with your own resources. Use your savings, any retirement accounts you can cash in, credit cards, second mortgages, and any personal belongings you can sell. Don't laugh: Most entrepreneurs have done the same thing to get their dreams off the ground. These personal sources of funds can count for a good chunk of your financial package.

Banks

Banks are really not all that great for getting money. They tend to be very conservative in their lending to assure their depositors that they are taking good care of business.

That means that they will only lend you money if they can be pretty sure they will get their investment back plus interest. It is possible, however, to get a bank to lend you money through the Small Business Administration (SBA). The SBA doesn't loan out money but rather guarantees up to 80 percent of the face value of the loan.

For excellent information on SBA loans and other tools to help you get started in any kind of business, check out the organization's website at **www.sba.gov**.

Leasing Equipment

Another possibility for funding at least part of your coffee house is to lease some or all of your restaurant equipment. Some restaurant equipment companies have information on leasing options, so start by contacting a local one. If there isn't one in your area, there are large companies that serve both the United States and Canada. Call any of them to receive a catalog of products and prices.

Here are a few suggestions to get you started:

- *KaTom Restaurant Supply, Inc.*
  www.katom.com
  Phone: (800) 541-8683

- *Superior Products Catalog Company*
  www.superprod.com
  Phone: (800) 328-9800

- *Rapids Wholesale Equipment Co.*
  www.4rapid1.com
  Phone: (800) 899-6610

Trades

In the restaurants I've been involved with, almost all of our advertising was done on trade. That means for every dollar we spent in advertising with a radio station, the radio station executives were allowed a dollar "in trade" to spend at our restaurant. You may be able to do the same thing with your accountant, lawyer, printer, newspaper, or anybody else you can think of. This will save cash up front and get people into your coffee house. Even if they are not paying cash, they will tell their friends if they like what they see (or taste), and this can help build business.

Sam Jones, owner of 2 Percent Jazz Espresso, is building a new coffee house. To save money, Sam is doing almost all of his construction on trade, including plumbing, electrical systems, cabinets, and even artwork!

You are still responsible for any taxes due on trades, so if you are going to do any trades, you will need to keep track of them. Give this information to your accountant so that they can take the appropriate steps to keep you in compliance with the proper taxing authorities.

Investors

If you can find someone who would like to invest in your coffee house, you need to strike a deal with them that doesn't give away your store. Investors are looking for a good return. If you pay them in monthly installments with an interest rate that is higher than they can get elsewhere, then that is good for both of you.

Avoid selling any equity in your business if you can. After six months, cash is probably not going to be as much of a concern. You don't want to be stuck with a partner you might not have needed. Better to keep the investment as a loan and sweeten the deal with some free coffee.

Family and Friends

Your family and friends will most likely be the people you turn to in the end. If you have worked out a deal with the landlord for some lease-hold improvements, traded where you can, and leased your equipment, the amount of money you need might not be that much. Family and friends will most likely make up a good chunk of the funds you still need to finish the project.

My family cosigned a $10,000 loan for my first restaurant. I had two partners, and they also put in $10,000 each. The landlord put in free rent for a period of time, our lawyer and accountant put part of their bills on trade, and we secured a small loan from the bank that owned the building. If it hadn't been for my folks taking the chance and cosigning on that loan, I wouldn't be writing this. Family can truly be a great resource.

Get Creative

All of this financial wriggling is why I believe so strongly in something that Paul Hawken said in his book, *Growing a Business:* "Money follows imagination; imagination never follows money."

Simply, this means that when you don't have money, you are forced to become creative and think of new ways to get yourself from A to Z. If you had buckets of cash to do anything you wanted, you might hire out all the thinking about design, buy the most expensive furniture, and so on. This could create delays in your opening and a larger monthly payment for the business. More money spent means less profit.

> **TIP:** If you can find one, choose an existing restaurant for your coffee house location. It will save you a bundle compared to building one from scratch, providing that the restaurant is not too old!

3. Setting Up Shop

3.1 Choosing the Right Location

For me, looking for business locations is pure fun. With each possibility, a whole future unfolds. When I see a building that looks like it would make a great location for a restaurant or coffee house, I can picture in my mind's eye what it will look like and how busy it might be. Once you get used to it, you will never stop looking for new spaces. Even after you are open, you will always be looking at other locations and wondering how a business would do there.

Many factors are involved in finding just the right location for your coffee house. They include the following:

- The look of the building

- Foot and car traffic

- Parking

- Crime

- The building's prior use

3.1.1 The Look of the Building

The look of the building is very important. Your business will have its own "look," and you will want the business and the building to complement each other. For example, an Italian coffee house would look better in an old brick building than in a strip mall. However, you can do some imaginative things to a strip mall exterior to accomplish a desired goal.

A space that has wood floors and high ceilings can go a long way toward making your coffee house feel comfortable. However, you also can do some creative things to a plain concrete floor and a drop ceiling to give your establishment a warmer feel. For example, you can paint the floor or create the illusion of high ceilings by painting the area above the acoustic tiles black. Some retail spaces just cry out for you to do something with them.

3.1.2 Foot and Car Traffic

J. Willard Marriott started out in the restaurant business in Washington, D.C. According to his biography, he and his wife, Alice, would park at an intersection of a possible restaurant location and use a clicker to count the number of cars that drove by. That way, he could get a sense of how busy the location would be.

When my partners and I built our first full-blown restaurant, we got information from the Chamber of Commerce. Their information stated that over 30,000 cars drove by our hopeful spot every day! No matter how you choose to do it, you should watch the location on different days of the week and at different times of the day, including at night, to get a feel for what kind of foot and car traffic will go by. Also, look at the people and ask yourself if you think they look like the type of people that would be your customers.

3.1.3 Parking

Is there parking close by or in the neighboring residential areas? In San Francisco, an excellent coffee house city, there is no such thing as parking "close by." Yet all the businesses are packed because people park in the residential areas and walk a couple of blocks.

In your town, people may not be accustomed to walking. If that's the case, you will want to provide plenty of parking. With most of the restaurants I've run, there wasn't much in the way of parking. In fact, it usually follows that if you have an interesting building, there isn't a lot of parking around because of the historical nature of the space. However, if the product you are serving is good enough, people will find a way to get to you.

For example, the café Downtown Subscription in Santa Fe started in a space with less than 1,000 square feet. The shop offered coffee drinks, toast, and more than 100 magazine and newspaper titles. They had no parking. However, they did have lots of foot traffic. When they expanded to a new location some years later, they lost their foot traffic but picked up a parking lot. The parking lot is always packed, and so is the café.

3.1.4 Crime

You may want to look at crime statistics for your area as well. If your customers are having their car CD players ripped off while enjoying an espresso at your place, you can bet they might not want to risk another visit. At one of our restaurants, we had problems with cars being broken into. We finally had to hire a security person to help our customers feel safer.

3.1.5 The Building's Prior Use

From my perspective, two of the biggest decisions in picking a location have to do with the space's prior use. Laws are different depending on where you live, but in most places, choosing a space that was previously a restaurant is much easier in many ways.

First of all, you are not changing use, so in most cases you will not need to have an architect submit plans before the city unless you are planning a major upgrade to the facility. Second, an existing restaurant space may already have a majority of the amenities you will need, like bathrooms that are up to code, floor drains, grease traps, and maybe some equipment such as an exhaust hood or a walk-in cooler. This can save you a bundle on the total cost of your coffee house. All of these items are expensive, and they are the kind of thing that customers can't see. Having this side of things taken care of frees up more money to spend on the things your customers can see, such as tables and chairs, light fixtures, and art.

Most of the restaurants that I opened were located on the sites of other restaurants that had failed for one reason or another. However, just because one restaurant fails doesn't mean the location is poor. My partners and I leased a restaurant space where the prior owner had spent over $800,000 to build it. We did an easy remodel and were in business for under $100,000. Nineteen years later, that restaurant is still in business and is very successful.

An existing restaurant space that is for lease will not only save you money but time as well (and some people say that's the same thing). With a restaurant space, you are only going to have do some simple remodeling and decorating. If your decorating needs don't require you to move any walls, you may not even need a building permit.

3.2 Building Your Coffee House

When you can't find a space that seems appealing, you may want to start fresh with a great space that has never been a restaurant before. In such cases, go with your instincts. If you are involved throughout the process, you can still finish on time and on budget. Should you choose to lease a space, you have the right to ask the landlord to contribute some money for a portion of the improvement costs. Owners are sometimes willing to do this because it improves their structure.

When building from scratch, I like to refer to the so-called Builders' Triangle. Each side represents either Fast, Cheap, or Right. You can have any two of the sides, but not all three.

In other words, something can be done:

- Fast and cheap, but not right

- Fast and right, but not cheap

- Cheap and right, but not fast

Leasing a Location for New Construction

If the building you're interested in is new construction, it is common for the landlord to give you a certain amount of money for the improvements — including expensive items like bathrooms. They may even be willing to do a complete buildout, as long as they know they will be getting their money back through lease payments.

If the landlord doesn't have the cash to put into the project, you can ask if they will abate the equivalent amount in rent over the period of the lease. It never hurts to ask the landlord not to charge you rent while you are under construction.

Purchasing a Location for New Construction

If you are in the position and can buy the location, talk to your lawyer and your accountant about it. They may recommend that you create a separate company to own the building and lease it out to yourself. It makes a lot of sense, tax wise, to do this. If the building is of historic value, it may be eligible for low-interest improvement loans. Most important, all the improvements you make to the property will be going into something you own.

Another great coffee house in Santa Fe is Café Oasis, owned by Toby Wilde and managed by Richard Kurtz. Richard has one great regret in the popular café, which has been in business since 1992: "If we had to do it all over again, we would own our own property."

Richard feels that renting the space for the past nine years has meant a lost opportunity to build value. While this is true, sometimes the best locations are not for sale, or you just don't have the capital to purchase it.

In spite of the fact that Richard has rented the property, Café Oasis has gained an excellent reputation based on their organic coffees and vegetarian meals. If Richard had decided not to rent, Santa Fe would be missing out on a great coffee house.

> **TIP:** Look in the "business opportunity" section of your local newspaper for restaurant spaces for lease or for sale. Also check with real estate brokers for spaces for sale or for lease.

3.2.1 Coffee House Design

When building your coffee house, the design and layout are as important as anything else. How the facility flows is vital to eliminating congested areas where customers tend to get stuck in lines or between tables.

While the possibilities are great no matter the size and shape of the building you choose, there are still certain rules you will want to follow regarding the placement of the counter, spacing of the tables, location of equipment, and so on.

In the following section, I will try to address some of these issues.

Traffic Flow

How customers enter and exit your coffee house is extremely important.

As much as possible, you'll want to avoid congesting areas with lines. Here are some specific guidelines:

Rule #1:

Place the ordering counter a sufficient distance away from the front door. This way, customers won't have to stand in a line that snakes outside. You will probably need a good 30 feet of space.

Rule #2:

Don't place the ordering counter in the center of the room. Instead, put it against the side wall. Your customers will automatically form a line against the wall and not get in the way of the tables in the middle of the room. This also saves more space for tables, and it frees up the back wall for displays.

Rule #3:

You need at least a 3-foot-wide aisle between the tables so that a wheelchair can get through. If you have a row of tables for two people (called "two-tops"), it's fine for the chairs that back up to each other to almost touch when people are sitting in them. However, there should be at least 3 feet to the side of the tables before another row of two-tops is located. This aisle will allow human traffic to flow by without disturbing the tables.

Rule #4:

Your countertop should be approximately 42 inches high. This is a comfortable height for resting an arm while ordering, and it is the typical bar height. The same rule applies for the back counter, or back bar. An exception would include a notch you could lower to make it easier for someone in a wheelchair to order from.

Rule #5:

There should be an 8-foot distance from the back wall to the front counter. This allows 2 feet for the back bar and any equipment that will go there, 3 feet for an open working area, and up to 3 feet for the front bar. Make sure the top surface of the bar hangs over the front of the bar by at least one foot, to give people sitting at the bar room for their knees.

3.2.2 Layout Specifics

For your basic coffee house bar, there are certain pieces of equipment you will want and need.

Bar Area

The following items are useful for your bar area:

- A hand sink, with a towel and soap dispenser.

- A three-compartment sink for washing glasses. If you are short on space, you can purchase or lease a commercial under-counter dishwasher.

- A reach-in cooler for juices, sodas, milk, and other beverages. You may also decide to put a refrigerated glass case in the front of the bar that could hold these items, as well as desserts.

- Built-in shelves to hold extra glasses and coffee cups. You can also store to-go bags, cups, and other miscellaneous items.

- An ice bin, which you may be able to get for free from your soda distributor.

- A soda dispenser and a place to keep syrups.

- A floor sink. This is a drain that looks like a sink but is flush with the floor. It goes under your three-compartment sink or dishwasher to catch spilled wastewater and keep it from coming in contact with the floor. Your local health department will require that you have one of these instead of a regular drain.

- Cleanable surfaces. The health department will want the walls and ceiling in your bar area to be of a light color and wipeable — which means no flat paints.

- Lights that are sealed behind a shield or have a rubber coating. The health department requires these lights to keep broken glass out of your food preparation materials. That way, if a light breaks, the broken glass stays behind the shield or the rubber coating holds the pieces together.

Restrooms

Building codes may vary regarding how many restrooms you need, but the number is generally based on how many customers your restaurant can seat. To be on the safe side, assume that you will need at least two.

If you took over an existing restaurant or coffee house, you may already have the restrooms in place. But contact your local health department or building department to check into codes concerning size and accessibility issues. As a general rule, your restrooms need to have a clear 5-foot circle once the door is closed so that a wheelchair can freely turn around. You will need a room that's at least 6 feet by 8 feet in order to accomplish this. Additionally, you will need a door that is 36 inches wide. If the restroom you inherited does not match this, then you will have some construction to do.

Inside the restroom, your toilet and sink have to be of a certain height. Codes are different, so consult with your building department to find out their exact requirements. Next to the toilet, you will also need a handrail for handicapped access. Any plumbing exposed under the sink needs to be wrapped and insulated (a person in a wheelchair may not be able to feel if their knee were being burned by a hot water pipe).

Above the toilet you will need a vent fan — preferably one that only goes on when the light is turned on, to save electricity. Other necessities include a toilet paper holder, paper towel dispenser, and soap dispenser. Unless you want something custom-made, you can get these dispensers from your main supply distributor. (See section 3.4 to find distributors.)

It is nice to have a mirror and plenty of light so that people can see themselves. It is also a good idea in the women's room to have a table for setting a purse down without having to place it on the floor. Another thing to include in both restrooms is a baby-changing station. You can get these from your regular supply distributor. They are made of a durable plastic and attach to the wall, but fold down for diaper changing.

Restroom Entrances

If you are building restrooms, keep the entrances out of view of the dining room. If they are already there and in view of the seating area, then try to position the doors to open in such a way as to block the view of the toilet. The reason is simple. People forget to lock the doors and someone will walk in giving full view to your other customers sitting down to their cappuccinos. It may seem like a small thing, but as long as you are building, you might as well save someone a lot of embarrassment.

Kitchen

Not all coffee houses serve food, but even if you only prepare muffins, you will need to have certain things in the back kitchen to make the health inspectors happy.

First of all, you will want walls that are light in color and washable. It's easier to tell if light walls are clean; if they're painted salmon, it's harder to spot dried food stains. You can make the walls easily washable simply by painting them with a satin or enamel finish. If you can afford it, you can purchase 4-foot by 8-foot Mylar sheets that can be glued to the wall. Mylar is nearly indestructible and will not rot when wet the way a painted wall will.

You will also need a separate mop sink. This is usually a square floor sink that measures 18 inches square and stands about 1 foot tall. It has no legs and just sits on the floor. Most health departments require one somewhere. It doesn't necessarily have to be in the kitchen, but that's generally the best place for it.

Additionally, you will need to have a grease trap. A grease trap sits in the floor and connects in-line with your wastewater pipes. The theory is that grease, which is heavier than water, gets caught in this trap before it flows into the sewer system, where it would coagulate and cause blockages further downstream. You can buy grease traps from a restaurant supply store such as Sysco or Superior Products. Your health department will let you know how big of a grease trap is required. If you are occupying an existing restaurant space, one is probably already installed.

Schedule to have your grease traps cleaned at least every six months. If you serve anything fried, have it cleaned once a month. Grease trap cleaning services are found under "Restaurant Equipment — Repairing and Servicing" in your local Yellow Pages.

The kitchen should have covered lights and a washable ceiling. If the kitchen is out of public view, then recessed fluorescent lights (the type you usually see in large office buildings) are the way to go. These provide plenty of light, and you can get them in their own box with a cover. If, however, your kitchen is open to the dining room, then you should use regular light bulbs that are easier on the eyes.

Under your dishwashing area, you will need a floor sink like the one in the bar. You may need an additional one if you also have a three-compartment sink for cleaning pots and pans.

Above the stove and oven, your kitchen should also have a hood, a make-up air unit, and a fire suppression system. The hood is usually a stainless steel box set against the ceiling above your cooking surfaces to catch all the steam and smoke from your cooking. It has a vent fan that draws the air up into it and removable screens that should be taken out every day and run through the dishwasher.

To compensate for all that air that is being sucked up through the hood, you will have a separate make-up air unit. This is a fan that draws fresh air from the outside at the same rate as air is sucked out through the hood. The hood and make-up air system are usually purchased as a single unit so the intake and output rates are already balanced.

The fire suppression system should be built into the hood. A typical fire suppression system has nozzles that stick down from inside the hood and point toward the cooking surface. Steel bottles behind the hood are charged with a fire suppression powder. If a fire in the stove gets out of control, heat sensors trigger the nozzles to let forth a whopping mess of powder all over your stove. You can usually purchase this system with your hood and make-up air.

There are independent companies who make these systems as well. You will find them in your local Yellow Pages.

Signage

One important marketing tool you'll want to have is a sign to identify your business to your customers. It should be large enough to be read easily from the street or sidewalk and have a design that's recognizable. It should announce your shop's name and could incorporate your shop's logo or a picture of a something coffee related. Use only a few, easy-to-see words, and keep it simple.

If your shop is located in a shopping mall or other managed property that already comes with a place to install a sign, you will probably be able to order an appropriate sign with the help of the property's management.

If you're on your own, professional sign companies offer design and manufacturing. Check in your local Yellow Pages under the "Signs — Commercial" category. You might also go through a local art school or contact local artists to see about doing a trade (free coffee once your shop opens in exchange for a logo and sign design).

Also be sure to check with your municipality regarding regulations that affect signage. Some places have rules that determine the size, placement, or look of signs. Take the design and description of your chosen sign to the municipal office to make sure it meets these standards.

Other Considerations For Your Layout

Sound System

When building, plan out your speaker wires for your sound system so that no wires will show. Have all wires run to your office and not to the bar area if you want control over the music being played. If the stereo system is behind the bar, your staff can slip their favorite CDs in when they get bored with your music selection, and you won't notice because you are in the back office counting the deposit. Trust me: This can be a problem. I speak from experience.

Nonslip Flooring

It's important to use nonslip flooring materials. In our first real restaurant, we had beautiful tiles that unfortunately were extremely slippery.

People went down on a weekly basis, until one day a nice lady lawyer slipped and fell, pointed her finger at us, and said to change the floor or she would sue. We knew she meant it, so we changed to a friendlier flooring material.

Wood is one of the nicest options. Carpet is the worst, because of staining. If you use tiles, get some that don't have smooth surfaces. It would help if you walked on them first to get a feel for what they would be like on your floor. Keep in mind that while you might be wearing running shoes, your business customers may be wearing dress shoes with no treads.

3.2.3 Choosing a Contractor

Many of the contractors I have used in the past were people I already knew. Who you pick to build your coffee house will determine when you will be able to open and how much money you will spend. Here are some things to look for when picking your contractor.

Collect Three Bids

Try to get at least three bids if possible. When doing this, it is important to compare apples to apples. In other words, make sure that your bids are off of the same set of plans. If you have hired an architect, you will be handing out copies of duplicate plans for contractors to bid on. However, if you are just remodeling an existing restaurant space, you have to be very careful when you explain what you want done to the contractor. You will need to repeat the exact same instructions to all the other contractors.

It helps to have this information in writing. If you are not careful, one contractor will suggest a better way of doing something in their bid, and then the next contractor will have a different way of doing something else. In the end, you will have three different bids on three different projects. Stick to your initial plan, at least for comparison. You can always go back and change things later once you decide which contractor you want to use.

Contractor References

When getting your bids together, be sure to ask each contractor for a list of references. Be sure to call all the references! This is one of your best resources for discovering the true qualities of the contractors.

When checking references, ask if you can go see the work that the person did. Even if you don't know much about how things are put together, at least you will have the satisfaction of actually seeing something that was built by the person. Usually, you can get a sense about the quality of the work. When talking to references, make a list of questions to ask each of them — and ask these same questions of each reference.

Here are some ideas:

- Was the work finished on time and on budget?

- Did the contractor do everything they said they would do?

- Did the workers clean up at the end of the day?

- Were there many change orders? (More on this below.)

- Were the contractor and crew boss pleasant to work with?

- Would you work with them again?

The more references you talk to, the better the overall impression you will have of the contractor. If the bids are close, this is an important part of deciding who will get the job.

Change Orders

Cost is not the only important consideration when picking a contractor. When checking references, find out how often there were change orders.

A change order is something extra you or the contractor suggest during the building process. Sometimes a contractor will bid low, knowing that he can make up the money by insisting on change orders. Remember, you did not bid on anything included in the change orders.

So when the contractor suggests a change order because they "didn't really know until they got into the walls," you need to take a moment to examine all of the alternatives. If you readily agree to the change order, keep track of the costs so that the final bill does not surprise you.

Most likely, it will be you who wants to change things once you get started. That's all the more reason to be sure of your plans before you start.

With one of our restaurants, I laid out the floor plan before I gave it to the architect to make it official. Before I did, however, I used masking tape to outline all the tables, chairs, and countertops on the bare floor. Next, I sat on a large ladder in the middle of the room so I could imagine how the traffic flow would work. I felt it was important to "see it." When the restaurant was built, it looked just like I had imagined it. No surprises.

Once you have hired your contractor, request a copy of their contractor's license and insurance coverage for your file. Contactors are required to have liability insurance and worker's compensation insurance.

Spending Time on the Job Site

As the building begins, spend as much time on the job site as you can. Be a part of the crew when it comes time to clean up at the end of the day. Bring in donuts and coffee, and get to know the crew boss and workers. The more they get to know you, the more they will want to see you succeed and the less likely they will be to take advantage of your checkbook (not that they would do this, but it just makes you feel better if the workers don't think of you as a nameless rich corporation).

The Walk-Through

As the big day approaches and your contractor is almost finished, you will do a walk-through with them and develop a punch list of all the small items that still need to be finished, fixed, or cleaned up. Once everything on the list is done, the contractor will get his final check.

Contractor Payments

For small jobs, contractors like to be paid half up front. On larger jobs, that figure can go down to 20 percent and then payments can be made weekly, semimonthly, or monthly until the project is completed. It is very rare that a construction company will hold off billing until the project is finished.

By the end of the project, you will hopefully be pretty close to all of the people who helped you. It is a good idea to invite them to your opening. These are your first goodwill ambassadors who will let the community know about you. It is time to start thinking of everyone as a potential customer.

3.2.4 Codes and Inspections

If you are building your coffee house, you will need a building permit, which you can obtain through your city or county building department. The building department will review your plans to make sure that everything is up to current codes.

If you hire an architect to draw up your plans, they should be up on all these codes and design your coffee house with them in mind. For instance, one code may require that your front door open to the outside rather than to the inside, so that in case of fire the door would open in the same direction as people would be moving to exit the building.

Other than the building department, you will also want to have your local health department look at the plans to see if they meet specific codes for food service operations. These would include things like proper lighting, washable walls, and available three-compartment sinks.

Call these agencies before you begin and ask for a preliminary inspection of the property. This will alert you early to any concerns the agencies might have in the project. It will also go a long way toward creating goodwill.

A building inspector will come out during the construction process to do an inspection when something is finished, such as the electrical rough-in. Once they inspect it, they will sign off on the building permit for what they just inspected. After everything is complete, the building inspector will do a final inspection and issue you a certificate of occupancy.

The health department will inspect you on an ongoing basis. How often this happens depends on where you live. Inspectors in Albuquerque came once a month; in Santa Fe it was once a year. However, when an inspector comes, it is always unannounced. That way, they are more likely to catch you if you are doing something that is against the rules, such as improper chemical storage. The health department will give you a rulebook and take the time to go over it with you so that you understand what is expected from you.

The health department also holds periodic classes in health and safety that are open to you and your employees. If such classes are offered where you live, I suggest you take them. It will help you to keep a cleaner, safer coffee house, and it will also let the health department know that you are serious about keeping a clean business.

3.3 Equipment and Supplies

3.3.1 Buying Equipment

To fill the space you have just built, you will need restaurant equipment. As I mentioned earlier, you may choose to lease a large amount of the equipment you will need. If you go this route, you will probably be going through one company. I recommend buying both used equipment and new equipment.

For used equipment, I like to pick durable pieces that are less likely to break. Here is a list of items that are easy to buy used:

- Stainless-steel prep tables
- Three-compartment sinks
- Pots
- Pans
- Cooking utensils
- Shelving
- Furniture

TIP: As soon as possible, start checking for used equipment in your local paper. Buy it and store it in your garage until you need it. If you wait until you do need it, you won't be able to find it used.

Here are some other items that you will need for your coffee house.

Baking Items

Mixers

If you are going to be baking, buy a used Hobart mixer. Hobarts are built like tanks. They have simple parts that are easy to fix. However, even when purchased used, they are not cheap. The largest mixer is the Hobart 60-quart, which when purchased used will set you back anywhere from $3,000 to $6,000. A used 30-quart mixer is a deal in comparison, sometimes costing as little as $1,500 or less. Which one you choose depends on the amount of baking you intend to do.

Certain attachments for the mixer are a must. You will need a dough hook for mixing dough, a wire whisk attachment for mixing dressings, and other attachments. An attachment for the front of the mixer would be a meat grinder. This comes with different blades for different uses. One blade is a cheese grater, which will allow you to grate a huge tub of cheese in about five minutes. Another one I recommend is the slicer attachment, which can be used for slicing vegetables like carrots and mushrooms. These are real time-savers and worth the bucks.

Ovens

There are many possibilities when it comes to choosing an oven. Whether you are baking only cookies or hearty Tuscan loaves, you need to choose the right type of oven for your needs.

Some of the simplest types of ovens are counter-top conveyor models. These operate by setting what you want to bake on a rotating conveyor belt that moves your baked item under an electric heat source, delivering the final product out the other side. This is a good oven for heating things up, but not one you would use for baking breads. They are usually referred to as impingers. Manufacturers include Blodget, Holman, and Lincoln. Costs run anywhere from $1,500 to $4,000.

Deck ovens are what you see in most pizzerias. They are recognized by their wide narrow doors. Inside is a simple floor or deck, that is made of masonry, which holds the heat and helps to firm up the bottom of the breads. They are durable and cheap. You can find used ones from $500 all over the place because of their proliferation in pizza joints. New ones cost from $800 to $5,000 depending on whether it is a single counter-top model or a freestanding double deck unit. Bakers Pride is the most typical manufacturer of these.

Convection ovens are the type you see in most coffee houses. They are simple in design, don't take up too much room, and bake fast. A convection oven operates by circulating heat inside the oven by way of a fan in the back. This movement of air speeds up the cooking process. Most convection ovens you see are made by Blodget and cost anywhere from $2,500 to $6,000. They operate off of gas or electricity, which makes these ovens very adaptable.

If you are serious about breads, I recommend getting a steamer oven. These look like convection ovens but operate by cooking with steam. It is the steam that will give breads their chewy crust. This was traditionally done by opening the door to your oven and misting the bread with water while it baked. With steamer ovens you do not need to do this. Steamers can run anywhere from $2,500 to $18,000. Doyan makes the best ones, though Blodget and Vulcan make good ones too.

Some convection ovens that Blodget makes also have steam as an option as well. This may be the way to go if you are not sure how much baking you will be doing. So when you are out shopping for used ovens, keep an eye out for convection ovens that also have a water attachment. This will indicate that steam will be available for your baking needs.

If you live in a cool climate, you will need a warm place to "proof" your breads before they are baked (proofing is another term for letting the dough rise). The easiest and most consistent way to accomplish this is to use a proofing cabinet. This is a tall metal cabinet that can be used to keep things warm, or in your case, to place sheet pans with dough for proofing. They come in all sizes and are on rollers so that you can move them around in your kitchen. Proofing cabinets are handy because you can place all your unbaked breads in them, turn them on, and the dough will rise or "proof" in a safe clean environment. Alto

Shaam and Metro make most proofing boxes. Prices vary from $1,000 to $6,000. However, you can usually find them used for around $500.

Refrigeration Equipment

Refrigeration equipment should be bought new. This includes your reach-in and walk-in coolers and ice machines. If you decide to buy a used cooler, however, find out how old the compressor is. (The compressor is the component that actually starts the refrigeration process when the thermostat reaches a certain temperature.) A new compressor costs around $500 and comes with a five-year warranty. That's about how long they will last in a commercial setting.

The other important parts to look at when buying a used refrigerator are the gasket seals on the doors and the condensing unit, which looks like a radiator with a fan. Make sure it's clean and not dented up.

Cash Register

The selection of a cash register should be taken seriously. You can go to a large discount store like Sam's Club or Price Club and get one for $100, but it will be very limited in what it can do. You'll want a register that has one button for every item on your menu. There are two reasons for this.

First, when a customer places an order, the person at the register only has to hit the item key and the total key. That's two keystrokes. If they had to look up a price, then key in the price, then hit the total button, that's four or more keystrokes. You may say, "I'm saving a few hundred dollars. I think people can handle a few extra keystrokes." Wrong! You will change your tune the first time there is a line at your register. In a coffee house, speed is everything. People hate to wait in line just to order a cup of java.

Second, a register that has a key for every item on your menu will also print out a report showing how many of each item you sold and at what time of day it was sold. This is useful information when adjusting the menu and trying to figure out food cost problems. For instance, if your food cost seems high, you can look at your report and see that 80 percent of your food sales are in cinnamon rolls that cost a lot to make. With this information, you can either raise the price of cinnamon rolls or start pushing items with a lower food cost to offset the high food cost of the cinnamon rolls. Remember: If you can't quantify it, you can't manage it. The information from your report can also be helpful for tracking customer preferences and buying habits.

Another important thing to keep in mind when shopping for a register is to get one with time-keeping capabilities. It is much more accurate if an employee can show up to work and clock in on the register rather than on a separate time clock. Since the register is basically a computer, it can give reports on how you are spending your labor and even combine them with sales to see if you are using your labor resources to their fullest capacity. You can even put the employees' schedules on the register so as to prevent someone from clocking in early or clocking out later than their shift without a manager override. This can save in a lot of costly mistakes.

Remote Printers

Many register systems have special features such as remote printers. The faster you can get the order to the person making the food and espressos, the faster you can serve customers. This increases your sales volume. If your kitchen is not right next to you, a remote printer can send the order to the cook, who can start making the item immediately. This eliminates the step of walking over and handing him the food ticket.

This is something to think about when you are laying out the floor plan of your coffee house. If you want to avoid buying a remote printer, it might make sense to have the espresso machine next to the register and have the kitchen just behind the register person.

Espresso Machine

At the heart of your coffee house, you will be making coffee. To research this section, I thought it best to consult with the person I lovingly call "The Godfather" of coffee, Bill Mehaffey of Bongo Billy's in Buena Vista, Colorado.

Bill says that no matter what type of espresso machine you buy, there are a few things to look for. "Look at the big coffee house chains and see what they are using," he advises. "You know that it must be a good machine to keep up with their volume. Also, you'll want to make sure that whatever machine you choose, it has a good warranty and a good history of dependability. If buying used, get a top-of-the-line machine like La Marzocco, La Cimbali (**www.cimbali.it**), or Rancilio (**www.rancilio.it**)."

Espresso makers are classified by the number of dispenser units, or "groups," that are built into the machine. Bill thinks that it is best to start with a two-group maker. You may get by with a single group, but if you have any sales volume at all, a single will not be able to keep up. A two-group can handle most volume levels. You would only go for a three-group if you were extremely busy.

The cost of a new two-group machine will run anywhere from $5,000 to $12,000. A used machine will be in the $3,000 to $5,000 range. Many of the espresso makers I have used have been manufactured by Astoria. These are pretty bulletproof machines, and there are plenty of them out there. I bought a used two-group, semiautomatic machine once for $1,200, and I got years of heavy use out of it.

To find your coffee equipment, I recommend using a company called EspressoPeople.com. Their website is full of all of the new coffee equipment you will need at reasonable prices. Take a look at the site to get a feel for what the equipment looks like and what the current prices are.

- *EspressoPeople.com*
  www.espressopeople.com
  Address: 588 Parsons Dr. Suite B
            Medford, OR 97501
  Phone: (888) 280-8584

Espresso Grinder

Bill recommends having two espresso grinders — one for regular espresso and one for decaf. The key with grinders is to make sure they have a durable, heavy-duty motor. A new espresso grinder will run from $700 to $900. Buying a used grinder may save you a few hundred dollars, but you may need to replace the burr (the part that does the actual grinding), which costs about $100.

Coffee Brewer

For your coffee brewer, there is no question that you want one that brews directly into an air pot. The old style of restaurant coffeemaker tend to "cook" the coffee as it sits on the burner. After 20 minutes, the coffee loses its freshness. A good choice is a thermal server to brew into. These servers have a pulse heat that keeps the coffee hot without burning it. A coffee brewer will run you around $600 to $800.

In addition to the brewer, you will want to attach a kitchen timer to the thermal pots. You will use this as a reminder that if the coffee in the thermal pot hasn't been used within a 1-hour period, it should be dumped and a new pot should be made. That will keep the coffee fresh, hot, and at peak flavor.

Dishwasher

When it comes to washing dishes, you have many choices. At Bongo Billy's, Bill uses a commercial version of a home dishwashing machine. The big difference between a home and a commercial machine is speed. Bill's machine is fast enough to keep up in his two busy cafés.

If your place is low-tech, all you need is a three-compartment sink (with 18 inches of drain board on both sides) and a person to lean over the sink to wash the dishes. You can find these sinks anywhere from $50 to $500.

Most high-volume restaurants use a dishwasher that sits in the middle of two stainless-steel tables with a sink and a long sprayer for rinsing dishes before they are loaded into the washer. The wash cycle lasts about two minutes. When the machine stops, you raise the doors, slide the dish rack out, and the dishes are ready to go again.

You can purchase these machines or lease them through different companies for around $140 per month. That price includes all maintenance and chemicals. I've always gone this way, and it hasn't been a problem for me. However, there is nothing wrong with buying a new or used machine and then just purchasing the chemicals separately.

Companies that specialize in dishwasher leasing include Auto-Chlor (**www.autochlorsystem.com**) and Sysco Foods (**www.sysco.com**).

3.3.2 Equipment Checklist

After buying as much used equipment as possible, you will then need to order the rest of your equipment new. To get you started, I've included a list of equipment you will need. This list is also included on the CD-ROM that comes with this book. You can use it as a checklist, and then add to it to suit your specific needs.

Equipment Checklist

Refrigeration

_____ Two-door reach-in cooler
_____ One-door freezer
_____ Walk-in cooler

_____ Sandwich prep table
_____ Ice machines

Electronics

_____ Stereo system
_____ Cash register
_____ Phone system
_____ Alarm system

_____ Credit card machines
_____ Calculator
_____ Computer

Equipment

_____ Stainless-steel prep table
_____ Dishwasher
_____ Two dishwasher tables
_____ Three-compartment sink
_____ Floor mixer (30 or 60 quart)
_____ Handheld mixer
_____ Tabletop mixer (KitchenAid)
_____ Food processor
_____ Slicer
_____ Range with oven
_____ Commercial hood with make-up air

_____ Wire rack shelves (metro shelving)
_____ Dunnage racks (stable racks to keep bags of flour on)
_____ Espresso machine
_____ Two espresso grinders (one for decaf, one for regular)
_____ Coffee brewer
_____ Two coffee grinders
_____ Two blenders
_____ Ice bin
_____ Fire suppression system

Furniture

_____ Tabletops
_____ Table bases
_____ Chairs
_____ Bar stools

_____ Countertops
_____ Two high chairs
_____ Two booster chairs
_____ Extra folding chairs

Supplies

_____ Window cleaner	_____ Assorted paper cups
_____ Bleach	_____ Paper thermal cup protectors
_____ General-purpose cleaner	_____ Paper cup lids
_____ Cleanser	_____ Cold drink cups with lids
_____ Green scrub pads	_____ To-go containers
_____ Steel wool	_____ To-go silverware
_____ Bar towels	_____ Paper bags
_____ Paper napkins	_____ To-go condiments
_____ Paper towels	(salt and pepper, sugar, etc.)
_____ Toilet paper	_____ Wooden stir sticks
_____ Aluminum foil	_____ Cash register paper
_____ Plastic wrap	

Small Equipment

_____ Sheet pans	_____ Small trash cans
_____ Assorted pots	_____ Ice scoops
_____ Stainless steel bowls	_____ Flour scoops
_____ Large sauté pans	_____ Commercial can opener
_____ Stockpot	_____ Water glasses
_____ Muffin tins	_____ Coffee cups
_____ Rubber spatulas	_____ Cappuccino cups
_____ Chef spoons	_____ Espresso cups
_____ Chef knives	_____ Silverware
_____ China cap (strainer)	_____ Salt and pepper shakers
_____ Assorted thermometers	_____ Sugar cruets
_____ Pastry bag with tips	_____ Silverware holder
_____ Flour bins	_____ Rubber floor mats
_____ Large trash can with wheels	_____ Vacuum coffee pots

3.4 Food Distributors

While your shop is under construction, various food distributors may get in contact with you. They seem to know about all the new places before they open. There are some pretty large food distributors out there who sell everything from breads and pastries to fully prepared meals that only need to be heated up. There may be smaller distributors in your area as well. The best way to find these distributors is to look in your local Yellow Pages under "Food Service Distributors." You'll find the big ones – Sysco (**www.sysco.com**) and U.S. Foodservice (**www.usfood.com**) – as well as smaller ones that are locally owned.

After you choose a few distributors, contact them to set up an appointment and fill out their credit application. Once their credit departments have approved your application, they will allow you to buy your inventory and will bill you weekly or every other week. While you are at your appointment, there are a few things you need to specify:

- You will not accept deliveries between 11:00 a.m. and 2:00 p.m. (lunchtime).

- You would like an updated price sheet weekly.

- Deliveries are to be checked in by a manager only. No dropping things off.

It is important that you are not receiving deliveries at your busiest times. You want to have the opportunity to make sure that the deliveries match what you ordered. Delivery drivers know who is watching inventory and who is not. While almost all drivers are professional and are the kind of people you will become friends with, some will deliver you short and sell your stuff off the truck to make a few extra bucks.

4. How to Run Your Coffee House

4.1 Beverages

4.1.1 Roasting Your Own Beans

Some coffee house owners roast their own beans. Roasting your own beans can be a particularly fascinating part of owning a coffee house. There are several advantages to going this route:

- The cost of green coffee beans is approximately half that of wholesale roasted coffee.

- Having a coffee-roasting machine visible to your customers is a subtle way of communicating the freshness of your coffee and your personal commitment to quality.

- By roasting your own coffee, you decide what kinds of coffee to make available by developing your own blends.

Roasting your own coffee is almost a business unto itself, and most successful coffee houses do not roast their own coffee. The decision is yours, but unless you have a passion to roast, I would put off roasting until you are very comfortable with your coffee house. But if you know you are interested in including a roasting operation in your coffee house, this section will help you get started.

Costs of Roasting

You must make serious considerations before you take the plunge and start roasting in your coffee house. While it is true that your green beans cost about half as much as finished roasted coffee, it can cost a great deal of money to get set up. You must include the cost of the roaster, the cost of hiring someone to roast the beans, the cost of keeping a large inventory of green beans on hand, and the cost of repairs to roasting equipment.

The two most common types of coffee roasting machines are a drum type roaster and a hot air roaster. Most people who roast on a small scale use the drum type, which is what we will use as our example.

A commercial coffee roaster is a fairly simple machine. Many types and sizes are available, from tabletop models that roast about 3 pounds per batch up to the size used by most small roasters, which does around 30 pounds per batch. Smaller models run around $5,000 to $7,000 used and up to $10,000 new. Larger machines run in the $10,000 to $15,000 range used or in the $20,000 to $30,000 range new.

The best places to look for coffee roasting machines include manufacturer's websites, commercial equipment suppliers, and advertisements at the back of coffee trade magazines (See the resources chapter at the end of this guide for a list of publications).

Some roasting equipment manufacturers include:

- *Diedrich Coffee Roasters*
  www.diedrichroasters.com
  Phone: (877) 263-1276
  Email: info@diedrichroasters.com

- *Loring Smart Roast*
  www.smartroaster.com
  Phone: (707) 526-7215
  Email: more.info@smartroaster.com

- *Ambex Roasters Inc.*
  www.ambexroasters.com
  Phone: (727) 442-2727
  Email: info@ambexroasters.com

CoffeeTec (**www.coffeetec.com**) also lists new and used equipment for sale.

In addition to the cost of the basic machine, you will need electrical and gas hookups, as well as venting. Depending on your town, you may also be required to add pollution control devices. You can purchase these extras from commercial coffee-roasting manufacturers.

If you own your roasting machine, you will want to have a thorough understanding of how the equipment is put together and how it can be fixed. If the drum fails to turn during a roast, you could lose a 30-pound batch of coffee. However, if you understand the mechanics of the machine, it is not difficult to stay on top of the maintenance. Included in this guide is a system for building an ongoing maintenance pro-gram for all of your coffee house equipment (see section 6.5).

You will either need to hire someone to do your roasting or learn how to do it yourself. Before you hire someone, think about whether you sell enough coffee to keep a full-time roaster busy all week. If not, consider hiring a part-time roaster or training one of your employees how to do it.

If you choose not to hire a roaster, you'll have to learn how to do the roasting yourself before you can train your employees to do it. Many equipment suppliers will include a training session with the sale of a new coffee-roasting machine. If you are lucky enough to find a used machine, then the training will have to be independent.

Either way, you should plan on attending a coffee-roasting school to learn not just about roasting methods and techniques but also about bean size, density and moisture content, and how these factors influence the roasting. You will want to learn the basics on how coffee is graded and what to look for when buying green beans. The school should also teach you the basics of cupping (discussed in a few pages), which is essential for evaluating different coffees.

Diedrich Coffee Roasters offers a two-day workshop at its facility in Sandpoint, Idaho, several times during the year. The workshop costs $250 and covers everything from how to purchase green coffee to understanding how weather conditions affect the roasting process. To find out more, visit **www.diedrichroasters.com/seminaroverview. htm**.

Boot Coffee also offers roasting and cupping workshops throughout the year. Three-day workshops cost $975. All are held at Boot Coffee's headquarters in Mill Valley, California. Visit **www.bootcoffee.com/ courses.html** to find out more.

Finally, the Specialty Coffee Association of America (SCAA) holds workshops at its annual conference. Registration fees vary depending on your membership status, although you do not need to be a member to attend. Visit **www.scaa.org/conference** for more infor-mation.

A Quick Guide to Roasting

As already mentioned, roasting your own beans can be a major undertaking, and you'll want to receive some instruction on how to do it. To get you started, here is some fairly detailed information.

Before you start your roasting session, you should know what type of coffee you want to roast. You should get out your log sheet, which is a written catalog you will keep that shows details about previous roasting sessions and the times, temperatures, and amounts you roasted. You'll also want to have a recipe sheet showing which beans will be used for your blends and the weights for each.

Next, you will turn on your roasting machine to let it warm up to approximately 400 degrees for the first type of bean you are going to roast. While the machine is warming up, you will weigh out your beans for each batch. If you plan on making a blend, you will not be roasting the blend all in one batch. Instead, you will roast each of the coffees individually that are to be used in that blend (each type of bean is roasted to its own unique style). Only after all of the beans have been roasted will you be ready to blend the coffee.

Then you will want to pour the beans into the hopper, which is the funnel on the top of the roaster. When you are ready with your stopwatch and the temperature is perfect, you will open the chute and let the beans flow by gravity into the drum, which is already turning. As the coffee gets roasted, the sugars and carbohydrates get caramelized, which create that oily look you see on finished beans. This is what gives coffee that great flavor and aroma. The longer you roast the beans, the darker they will get. But before they start to take on the look of finished coffee, they will go through a series of changes.

In the front of the roaster is a small sample scoop that can be withdrawn in order for you to visually inspect the coffee as it is roasting. The scoop is open on one side and is kept in the drum with the open side facing down so that beans don't collect in the scoop and miss out on the roasting. When you pull a sample, you turn the handle facing up to collect an amount of beans, pull it out, inspect the beans, push the handle back in and turn it again so that the open end is again facing in the down position. (This entire process takes about two seconds.)

In the first three minutes of roasting, the beans will give off a grassy fragrance. Then they will begin to swell up and change from green to yellow to gold. By the 9-minute mark, the beans will have begun to wrinkle.

Next, gases build up inside the bean, which makes them swell up to twice their original size. This causes them to pop as the gas escapes. It's important to note the exact time of the "first pop" on your log sheet, as the pop time will be different for each type of coffee. The swelling is important because it smoothes out the wrinkles on the surface of the bean. Now at about 10 minutes, after the first pop has occurred, the color of the bean will begin to even out, turning a light brown. This stage is referred to in the industry as a "cinnamon roast."

Now the process speeds up. You really have to be on your toes, as seconds count toward roasting the perfect batch of coffee. At 11 minutes, the color of the bean changes to a darker brown, which is commonly known as "Full City." By 12 minutes, gases build up again and you will hear a second pop. Depending on what type of roast you are after, you may want to stop at this point. By the 15-minute mark, your beans will have become very dark. This is known as "French Roast," which is basically the same as an "Espresso Roast."

Once you have determined the perfect roast for your coffee, you will open the door to the drum and the beans will spill out onto the round collection table, which is part of the roaster. This table has a perforated screen on the bottom to let air pass through and a series of rakes that turn to spread the beans, allowing them to cool as quickly as possible. This cooling will stop the cooking process.

The collection table can also be used to blend the beans. After roasting, weigh out your beans according to your blend recipe and add them to the mixing table. The rake will do a good job of evenly mixing the different beans together. After mixing, your blend is ready to bag.

Cupping

If you are a coffee enthusiast, you are probably aware of the idea of cupping. This is where people take a spoon full of coffee and slurp it very loudly to determine the coffee's quality. Of course, it is more complicated than that. The purpose of cupping coffee is very scientific, and is an excellent way to determine the quality of coffee and help you create your own blends.

The best way to learn how to cup is by attending cupping sessions given by roasters and coffee brokers. However, you can also teach yourself to cup.

First, place 2 tablespoons of coarsely ground coffee into a 6-ounce mug. Don't add water yet; instead, breathe deeply and inhale the aroma of the fresh grounds (called the "dry aroma"). Note your impressions.

Add boiling water to the coffee, then wait 3 minutes. A crust of coffee grounds will form at the top of the cup. Using a clean spoon, break the crust and stir the coffee. Skim the foam off the top of the cup and throw it away.

Wait until the coffee has cooled enough to taste it and all of the grounds have sunk to the bottom of the cup. Then, with your spoon (which you should rinse after skimming the foam), take a small sip of coffee and slurp it into your mouth. Slurping the coffee will spray it evenly across the inside of your mouth, rather than having it make contact with only one point. Swish the coffee around inside your mouth and think about how you would describe the coffee's quality.
Pay attention to these attributes:

- Acidity: Is the coffee dry or tart? Does it taste winey or citrusy?

- Body: Does it feel "heavy," like cream, or "light," like skim milk?

- Aroma: Does it smell rich or weak?

- Flavor: What words describe the overall taste of the coffee? Sour? Sharp? Burned? Woody?

You can use cupping to compare different types of coffee at the same time. Just follow the steps above, but use a different cup for each type of coffee and make sure you rinse the spoon between each step.

You can watch some short cupping demonstration videos at **www.coffeeresearch.org/coffee/cupping.htm**.

Buying Green Beans

As a coffee roaster, you will be buying unroasted, green coffee beans. You should buy these beans from a variety of coffee brokers. Each coffee broker represents a geographic area of the globe where coffee is produced, and, as mentioned earlier, geographic location affects the flavor of the beans.

The price of coffee will depend on many factors. For one thing, it will depend on world coffee commodity prices, which are affected by demand, production, quality, the purchase power of the dollar, and coffee futures pricing. As you can see from this list, there is a good chance that the price will be different every time you buy coffee.

Depending on your commitment to purchase, some brokers will let you lock into a set price. You can buy small amounts of coffee, which will keep your inventories low and keep less of your cash locked up in unroasted coffee. Coffee is cheaper by the pound when purchased in large quantities; however, doing this will tie up a lot of your capital in inventory. I recommend going with smaller orders until you get a feel for how fast you will go through your stock. Once you are comfortable with your volume, you can commit to larger orders to get better price breaks.

Some coffee brokers include:

- *Chew Brokers, Inc.*
  www.chewbrokers.com
  Phone:　　(800) 311-7692

- *ProCoffee*
  www.procoffee.com
  Phone:　　(800) 803-7774
  Email:　　sales@procoffee.com

- *West Coast Specialty Coffee*
  www.specialtycoffee.com
  Phone:　　(650) 259-9308
  E-mail:　　rh@specialtycoffee.com

If unroasted coffee beans just sit around, they generally will not go stale. Coffee freshness is usually measured from the time the coffee is roasted until it is ground and brewed. Ideally, that time should be within seven days.

4.1.2 Brewing Coffee

A great cup of coffee requires the right coffee, brewed at the right temperature, in the right amounts, with the right equipment. Read on to find out how to make sure every cup of coffee you serve is a great one.

Grind

If your coffee is ground very finely, more of its surface area will come into contact with the hot water inside the brewer. This will result in a richer flavor. However, if the coffee is ground too finely, it will cake and the brewing water will not penetrate, making the brewed coffee very weak. Try to use the finest grind you can without causing your coffee to suffer.

Quantity

Most vacuum pots – those push-button, pumpable coffee dispensers – hold about 2.25 quarts of liquid. To brew that amount of coffee, use about 3 to 4 ounces of coffee per 2.25 quarts of water. Depending on the size of brewer you decide to get, you will have to do the math and adjust this amount. Then you will need to taste a lot of coffee to get just the right taste for you and your customers.

Temperature

Brewing quality coffee requires your coffeemaker to brew at the right temperature. Generally speaking, this is 196 degrees Fahrenheit. Water that is too hot will scald your coffee and make it bitter. Water that is too cold will not release the coffee's full flavor.

To test your machine out, place a thermometer under its water outlet and run the machine with no filter basket added. If the water coming out is less than 193 degrees or more than 198 degrees, you need to adjust the temperature setting. This usually needs to be done by the manufacturer or someone else who is qualified to work on brewers. On some coffee brewers, a manual lever allows you to make adjustments yourself, but check your owner's manual before proceeding.

Water

It is best to use filtered water in your brewer. You'll want to filter out any chlorine or off flavors from your tap water. It is generally cheaper to buy a filtering system for your brewer than to have special bottled water to use for coffee, although I have seen this done.

Age

Don't let the brewed coffee sit around too long. (Two hours qualifies as too long.) If you are using one of those old-fashioned hot plates to keep a pot of coffee warm, then 20 minutes is too long, because the coffee is cooking the whole time. I recommend that you buy an audible kitchen timer that can be attached to each vacuum pot of coffee and that you set the timer to 90 minutes. When the timer goes off, pour the unused coffee down the drain and start with a fresh batch.

You will soon learn how much coffee to have on hand so that you minimize waste. If coffee sits too long in a vacuum pot, it will lose heat, and without a doubt, your customers will hate drinking lukewarm coffee!

4.1.3 Espresso Basics

An espresso machine brews coffee by pushing hot water through a screen at high pressure, as opposed to a drip coffee machine, which brews by gravity. Making espresso involves three main steps: grinding, brewing, and steaming. You need only one machine to do all of this, and you will learn all you need to know about operating it by reading the instruction manual. However, here are some additional tips that you may find useful.

Grinding

The proper grind will determine the color and the texture of your coffee. You can test the grind by pressing the grounds firmly in your hand until it forms a cake. The cake should be firm but then fall apart easily.

A grinder has a hopper on top of it for whole beans. When the grinder is turned on, the beans flow from the hopper into the grinder and then out into the ground coffee holder. An adjustable ring at the base of the hopper will allow you to select a finer or coarser grind. Make sure this ring is off-limits to your staff so that your grind will remain consistent. However, don't leave the ring alone. You will find that weather changes, such as changes in humidity, will determine whether you need a tighter or a looser grind.

Brewing

The proper amount of time to fill an espresso cup (which usually means about halfway full) is approximately 20 seconds. If the coffee comes out of the machine in slow drips, it means the grind is too tight or there is too much coffee in it. This will result in a burnt taste. If the coffee comes out too rapidly, it means the water is either going through too course a grind or is going around the coffee, which will result in a bitter flavor. When the espresso comes out correctly, there will be a nice, foamy, coffee-colored "head" that appears slightly oily.

Steaming

To properly steam milk, you need a cold stainless-steel pitcher and cold milk to steam. If your liquid is too warm, you will not get an adequate amount of froth.

Start by releasing a little steam to make sure the steaming wand (the stainless-steel tube that sticks out from the espresso maker) is clear of any old milk. Then insert the wand just under the surface of the milk and turn on the steam fully.

Adjust the pitcher so that the steam wand is just at the surface. Much like how the water in your tub creates the most bubbles in a bubble bath where the water hits the surface, the moving action of the steam wand at the surface of the milk will create the most foam. If the wand is at the bottom of the pitcher, it will also make foam, but not as quickly.

As the foam is created, the volume expands, and you'll need to adjust the position of the pitcher to compensate. When you have achieved the amount of foam you need, plunge the wand to the bottom of the pitcher to heat the rest of the milk or soy.

As the milk steams, it forms three distinct layers: hot liquid, a thicker creamy froth, and foam, which has a lot of bubbles but is not as creamy. You can get to the hot liquid by holding a spoon to the spout to hold back the foam, allowing only the liquid through.

The easiest way to get the froth out is to just pour the contents into the cup. If you only want the foam, just spoon it out from the top of the steaming pitcher. If you let the pitcher stand and cool for 30 seconds, the foam will firm up, and you can spoon it out in great wisps like a meringue. Depending on what type of drink you are making, you'll add the foam in different ways. For example:

- A cappuccino requires a shot of espresso topped with a little steamed milk and mostly foam.

- A café latte is a shot of espresso with a lot of steamed, frothy milk.

- A café au lait is regular brewed coffee with half-and-half and steamed, frothy milk.

A note about milk: Gone are the days when there was just plain milk. Now you can choose between whole milk, 2 percent, low-fat, and skim. Milk can also be regular or organic.

It is a myth that you need a large butterfat content in milk to get a thick and rich foam. In fact, skim milk foams better than whole milk. If a customer is allergic to milk, you can offer soy milk or rice milk. Soy milk steams just as well as regular milk, while rice milk does a decent job but isn't quite as good.

Your customers will tell you soon enough what they prefer. I would suggest, however, that you at least start with a selection of whole, skim, and soy milk.

4.1.4 Specialty Coffee Drinks

The number of specialty coffee recipes you can come up with is almost unlimited. This section includes a few ideas you can use for your own coffee menu. You can then start to experiment with some of your own tastes and get as creative as you like.

I think it's fun to make up coffee drinks that have something to do with your own location. For example, the area where I live in western Colorado is known for its peaches. So I invented a drink called a Peach Kick. Depending on where you live, you may come up with something truly wild. You can make up your own names and variations.

Almond Joy

Ingredients:

- 1 or 2 shots of espresso
- 3 ounces of chocolate syrup
- 3 ounces of coconut milk, or 1 teaspoon of coconut syrup
- 4 ounces of milk — whole, skim, or soy
- 1 teaspoon of almond syrup
- 3 cups of ice

Instructions:

Blend and serve in a pint glass with whipped cream and shaved chocolate.

Bride of Frappuccino

Ingredients:

- 1 or 2 shots of espresso
- 3 ounces of chocolate syrup
- 1 teaspoon of vanilla syrup
- 4 ounces of milk — whole, skim, or soy
- 3 cups of ice

Instructions:

Blend and serve in a pint glass with whipped cream and shaved chocolate.

Peach Kick

Ingredients:

- 1 whole skinned pitted peach (fresh or frozen)
- 1 shot of espresso
- 1 cup of ice
- 6 ounces of milk — whole, skim, or soy
- 2 teaspoons of sugar or honey

Instructions:

Blend and serve in a pint glass with a peach slice.

Cowboy Coffee

Ingredients:

- 3 tablespoons of ground coffee in a French press
- 8 ounces of water at a full boil (or use water from espresso maker)

Instructions:

The coffee will come to the surface. Serve it with a spoon so the customer can sink the coffee that forms a crust on the surface. This one will take some customer education on your part, but it will be fun, and the coffee is excellent.

Depending on the type of coffee house you decide to open, you may be able to get a liquor license as well. It depends on your local regulations. For example, in New Mexico, a full liquor license is a limited commodity that can be bought and sold, so the typical price runs as high as $200,000 to $300,000! In Colorado, state fees run about $1,000 per year.

If you are able to get a full liquor license for your coffee house, there are some other specialty coffee drinks that you can make that may enhance your business into the night, especially if you also have a music venue.

Irish Coffee

Ingredients:

- A shot of espresso, or straight drip coffee
- A shot of Irish whiskey
- One tablespoon of regular or brown sugar
- Whipped cream

Irish Mocha

Ingredients:

- Irish Cream
- Hazelnut syrup
- Dark mocha
- Whipped cream
- Shaved chocolate

Midnight Mint

Ingredients:

- Peppermint Schnapps
- Dark mocha
- Whipped cream
- Shaved chocolate

Harbor Night

Ingredients:

- Rum
- Espresso
- Hot water
- Brown sugar
- Whipped cream

The key to a lot of these drinks is to have a line of specialty syrups. There are different types, such as Torani, Dolce, and Routin. I especially like Torani because not only are the syrups good, but the labels are attractive and a row of them behind the bar makes for a neat impression.

Another area where you can get creative with your specialty coffee drinks is in how you garnish them. It's good to have mocha with shaved or sprinkled chocolate to put on top of the whipped cream, but try other garnishes as well. For example, the Peach Kick gets a slice of peach, while the Harbor Night might get a slice of banana. The Almond Joy might be good with sprinkled coconut on top.

A huge head of whipped cream is impressive, but sprinkle a little cinnamon on top, and it will really stand out.

Thanks to Starbucks and other chain coffee houses, more and more people are trying types of coffee drinks other than drip coffee, cappuccinos, and lattes. However, the small independent coffee houses that do not need corporate permission to try some new flavor combination can really push the envelope. This is what makes independent coffee houses so unique. So have a good time playing with flavors, and let your imagination fly!

4.1.5 Other Specialty Drinks

In addition to your coffee drinks and specialty coffee drinks, you will want to have a good selection of drinks that are not coffee related. Again, the possibilities are almost endless, but I've included some ideas you can use to include in your menu.

Teas

- **Chai Tea:** Served hot or cold, this drink is a must. You can buy it ready made, so all you have to do is to steam it or pour it over ice and you are done.

- **Mango Tea:** This is ice tea with mango in it. You can get this from your tea provider. It is very refreshing!

Two great places to purchase tea wholesale are SOMA (**www. somatea.com**) and Tea Affair (**www.tea-affair.com**).

Smoothies

Try these combinations, and make up your own names for them. For some, you may choose to use just fruit, while for others, you can add protein powder, bee pollen, spirulina, or other interesting things.

- Mango nectar, coconut milk, and ice

- Strawberries, apple juice, banana, yogurt, and ice

- Blueberries, honey, bee pollen, apple juice, and ice

- Peaches, strawberries, protein powder, yogurt, and ice

- Chocolate milk or chocolate soy, strawberries, bananas, and ice

Sodas

It is a good idea to serve a line of interesting sodas as well. Many sodas come in decorative bottles, which will look good on your shelf. There is no need to serve boring, mainstream sodas when there are plenty of other options. If you have a natural grocery store in your area, look at what kinds of sodas they are selling. It is quite possible that some of them are made locally.

And speaking of local sodas, why not make your own? It is not hard, and it can become a real signature item for you. To make your own soda, you need only a few items:

- A soda keg

- A CO_2 tank and regulator

- Connecting hoses

- A keg cooler

- Raw ingredients for the soda

You can purchase these items from food service distributors and home brew equipment suppliers such as Cellar Homebrew. Visit **www. cellar-homebrew.com** to see what they have to offer.

Soda flavoring costs around a dollar per ounce. However, each ounce of flavoring yields a gallon of soda (128 ounces). If you sell 12-ounce glasses of soda for $1.75 each, you can make $19.25 (minus the initial dollar for the cost of the flavoring) per gallon. That's a heck of a profit.

You can be creative with your recipes as well. Try adding honey into the sugar mix, or try using spices. You can use root beer to make floats or other specialty drinks.

Needless to say, there are many possibilities for specialty drinks to serve in your coffee house. Start small with your choices so that they stay manageable. Once you are comfortable with your operation, you can expand your selection. Your customers will certainly be glad you did.

4.2 Food

4.2.1 Menu Planning

In our first coffee house, we sold coffee and cookies out of a 100-square-foot space. Eventually, our menu evolved into a full-blown Italian menu of sandwiches, soups, salads, baked goods, and specialty desserts, which required a larger location. Your coffee house will probably fit somewhere in between these two extremes.

Types of Food to Sell

At the heart of it, there is no set rule on how much food a coffee house needs to sell or if it should sell any food at all. You will most likely find, however, that your customers will want something to go along with their coffee or tea.

If you choose to sell food, the size of your menu will depend on your personal experience and comfort level with food service. If you don't have a solid restaurant background, keep the menu as simple as possible.

For ideas on how to do this, talk to your food suppliers (see section 3.4 for more about finding suppliers) about what types of foods they sell that are ready to go or that just need to be finished off in your oven. This will keep your food preparation to a minimum and your product consistency strong. You can keep the menu down to some baked goods like cookies, sweet rolls, and maybe a couple of great sandwiches.

On the other hand, if you do have a solid background in food, make your menu interesting and quality driven. I like to steal ideas, and when I steal ideas, I only steal from the best. Look to the great coffee houses and see what they sell, then try to come up with something better.

Menu Design

Design your menu to highlight the items you want to sell most. People usually look at the top, bottom, and middle of the menu first before examining all the choices. The items you want to sell the most of should be placed in those areas. This can have a great effect on the success of your menu.

The menu should be clear and easy to read. If you have a lot of unfamiliar or hard-to-pronounce names for menu items, then number them. That way, if a person cannot pronounce what they want, they can at least ask for "Number 12."

You may find that many of your customers are older and that their eyesight isn't what it used to be. Because of this, make sure the lettering on your menu is large and easy to read. The sample menu below is included on the CD-ROM. You can use it as a starting point to create your own menu.

Sample Menu

Coffee Drinks

Brewed Coffee	12 oz.	$1.25	16 oz.	$1.50
Café au lait *(coffee with milk)*	12 oz.	$1.50	16 oz.	$1.75
Espresso	Single	$1.25	Double	$1.75
Americano *(diluted espresso)*	Single	$1.25	Double	$1.75
Cappuccino *(espresso, foam, steamed milk)*	Single	$2.00	Double	$2.50
Café Latte	Single	$2.00	Double	$2.50
Café Mocha	Single	$2.25	Double	$2.75

(Ghirardelli chocolate, espresso, steamed milk, foam)

Non-Coffee Drinks		Extras	
		Flavored syrup	.50
Pot of Tea	$1.50	Soy milk	.50
Chai Latte	$2.75		
		Baked Goods	
Smoothie	$3.00		
(Flavors: banana,		Coffee Cake	$1.75
orange, cider, berry)		Muffin	$1.50
		Scone	$1.50
Italian Soda	$2.25	Cookie	$1.00
(syrup, soda, cream)		Breakfast Bar	$1.50
		Cake	$1.75
Milk	$1.00	Pie	$1.75
		Cinnamon Roll	$2.25
Hot Chocolate	$1.50		

Larger Plates

1.	Soup of the Day	$3.50
	(served with French bread and butter)	
2.	Garden Salad	$2.25
3.	Pasta Salad	$3.50
4.	Spinach Salad	$3.50
5.	Chicken Salad	$4.50
6.	Tuna Salad	$4.50
7.	Tuna Salad Sandwich	$4.95
8.	Sliced Turkey Sandwich	$4.95
9.	Chicken Salad Sandwich	$4.95
10.	Veggie Sandwich	$3.95

Food Cost

A menu not only has to be good, it also needs to make money. What I am referring to is your food cost. A good menu should have an average food cost of 25 percent. That means if you sell a sandwich for $4.95, it should only cost you $1.24 to make. That's just for the cost of the food and doesn't include labor or anything else.

So when you plan a menu and you have a target food cost of 25 percent, you will want to plan on having each item cost a little less than 25 percent of your sales price for you to make. That way, you have some breathing room to account for waste and theft.

To come up with a price, simply figure out the actual cost of all the food items that go into making the recipe. Then take that number and divide by your desired food cost. In the example above, the cost of the sandwich is $1.24. Take that amount and divide by what you want as a food cost (in this case, .25) and you will get the price you need to sell that item at: $4.95.

Some items may be too expensive if you use this formula across the board. Keep the amount of menu items that do not meet your desired food cost to a minimum. What works best is to have the items that will be your biggest sellers account for at least 80 percent of your food sales.

For these items, try to cost them out around 15 percent. Then you can have some items on the menu that are more expensive to serve and could cost as much as 30 percent or more. This enables you to offer some great value in the more expensive items and still come out with an overall food cost of 25 percent.

Keep in mind that these food costs are only suggestions. You may find that your total overhead for your coffee house is so low that you can afford a higher food cost. Perhaps your overhead is so high that you need a much lower food cost than the one I suggest to boost your profits to pay for the higher rent or bank note.

Controlling menu food costs is where having a cash register that tracks individual food sales really comes in handy. (You can find out more about cash register options in section 3.3.1.) If at the end of the month you calculate a food cost that is too high, you might find that you are selling too many high food cost items and not enough low-cost ones. Armed with that information, you can quickly change the menu and improve your food cost.

4.2.2 Sandwich and Soup Basics

Soups

In addition to baked goods, your coffee house menu should probably have a selection of sandwiches and soups. The reason is simple: They are easy to prepare, and appropriate for lunch and dinner.

If you have never been in the restaurant business before, you may wonder where to begin designing a line of soups and sandwiches. Hopefully, this section will take some of the mystery out of preparing these basic food items.

In my first restaurant, we served up a different soup every day. Making 5 gallons of fresh soup requires only a few basic ingredients and a few optional ones. If you would like to have a soup that changes daily, here is a basic recipe for any kind of soup:

Basic Soup Recipe

1. Finely chop 5 yellow onions.

2. In a 5-gallon stockpot, sauté onions in 8 oz. of butter — preferably unsalted. Cook until onions become translucent.

3. Add optional ingredients (vegetables, meat, etc.) until pot is filled to the 30 percent to 40 percent mark.

4. Add 4 gallons of stock.

5. Add salt and pepper to taste.

6. Let simmer for two hours.

7. When finished, ladle soup into a blender and blend at high speed. If cream soup is desired, add half-and-half cream before blending.

8. Pour blender contents into serving pot.

9. Garnish as desired.

Now, that was simple. But that's my point. Making soup is very simple and open to your own interpretation. So don't be afraid to try new things.

For instance, if you want to make potato leek soup, follow the recipe above and add two bunches of chopped leeks, one stalk of celery, and chopped potatoes in Step #3. Garnish with chopped fresh leek.

To make the stocks, just follow the directions on the carton for the concentrated stock variety. Vegetable, beef, fish, and chicken are all available from your food supplier in concentrated form. This is the easiest to work with.

Here is a completed recipe for Minestrone Soup. It is an all-around favorite. If you look closely at the recipe, you will see that it is just a variation of the simple soup-making method on the previous page.

Minestrone Soup Recipe

1. Finely chop 5 yellow onions.

2. In a 5-gallon stockpot, sauté onions and 2 cups of pureed fresh garlic in 8 oz. of butter — preferably unsalted. Cook until onions become translucent.

3. Add the following:
   1 lb. vegetarian soup base
   1 10 oz. can diced tomato with juice
   1/2 cup dry oregano
   1/4 cup dry basil
   4 bay leaves
   4 cups tomato paste
   4 gallons of water

4. Bring pot to a boil.

5. Turn off heat, then add:
   4 boxes of fiesta blend frozen vegetables or equivalent amount of fresh vegetables
   1 lb. cooked corkscrew pasta
   1/4 cup salt
   1/8 cup black pepper

6. Adjust seasonings to taste. Do not boil again, as vegetables will overcook.

7. Cool in ice bath in small batches.

8. Label, date, and store.

Sandwiches

If you thought the possibilities were limitless for soups, you'll be happy to learn that there are just as many possibilities for sandwiches. Not only do you have a wide variety of ingredients, but you also have options when it comes to hot or cold sandwiches, open-faced or closed sandwiches, and the type of bread you use.

To keep things basic but still interesting, we will concentrate on one type of hot sandwich that you can serve because it is a quality product, it is easy to prepare, and I guarantee it will be a cut above anything else that is being served out there.

Bread is a tricky issue in making sandwiches. Everyone has their own favorite type of bread, so I say offer just one kind, but make it unique and good. This will make it much easier than having to inventory a whole bunch of styles. I like to use focaccia because it is Italian bread –a perfect fit for a coffee house–and it makes a really great sandwich.

I also like to use a sandwich press, which is similar to a waffle iron. The sandwich gets pressed inside two hot surfaces and cooks for two minutes, and it comes out nice and hot with good-looking grill marks on the bread. Most customers would much rather have a hot sandwich than a cold one anyway.

If you have a bakery in your town, they can make your focaccia for you. Many major food distributors, such as Sysco, have excellent ready made products you can use. If you have an oven and a large mixer, you can also make your own bread.

One simple recipe for focaccia appears on the next page. This bread will wow your customers with its full flavor and freshness. Combine this with cooking the sandwich in a sandwich press, and you will have a memorable meal.

You can put almost anything in this sandwich and cook it in the press and it will be terrific. However, there are a few things to include in a sandwich that will make it great. First, some sort of cheese is a must on all kinds of sandwiches (unless you are preparing a vegan sandwich). In addition, a sauce or spread is needed, or the sandwich will be too bland.

Homemade Focaccia

Yield: One batch, or two large sheet pans

1. Sauté one yellow onion, finely chopped, in a small amount of olive oil until onion is translucent.

2. Add 1/2 cup of fresh rosemary.

3. In large dough mixer, mix 2 1/2 quarts of warm water with 1/2 cup of honey.

4. Add 1/2 cup of yeast and let stand until yeast is active.

5. Add 1 cup of garlic olive oil and mix on lowest speed.

6. Slowly add mixture of 8 quarts flour and 1/3 cup of salt.

7. When mixture comes together, add onion and rosemary mixture.

8. When dough forms a ball, continue mixing for 10 minutes to knead.

9. Transfer to clean container, cover, and allow to rise for 30 minutes.

10. Spray two sheet pans with oil, and spread dough out evenly on them.

11. Brush lightly with olive oil and Parmesan cheese, and dimple with fingers.

12. Bake in oven at 375 degrees for 15 to 20 minutes or until crust becomes golden brown.

13. Take bread out of the oven, remove from sheet pans, and let cool for 30 minutes.

14. Cut into sandwich-sized pieces, and store in Tupperware box.

One easy spread is mayonnaise. You can mix almost anything to make the mayo more interesting. Pesto makes a good mix, as well as sundried tomatoes. You can also use olive oil in place of mayonnaise or some other sort of infused-flavor oil, such as hot chile pepper oil.

Here are some sandwich ideas that you can use as a baseline for your own sandwich creations:

- Marinated eggplant with roasted red bell pepper and Monterey Jack cheese

- Fresh mozzarella, roma tomatoes, and fresh basil, with extra virgin olive oil spread

- Grilled chicken breast, smoked bacon, roasted red bell pepper, and fontina cheese with pesto mayonnaise

- Turkey breast, roma tomatoes, arugula, and mozzarella with sun-dried tomato mayonnaise

- Prosciutto ham, pepperoni, mozzarella, red onion, and pepperoncini peppers with Dijon mayonnaise

To come up with more ideas for sandwiches, pay attention to what other restaurants are offering. Most of our own innovative ideas came from inspiration that we found by visiting other restaurants. We used to take trips to San Francisco and visit up to 20 restaurants per day — no kidding. We wouldn't eat in them all. Sometimes we would have an appetizer or a drink, and other times we just popped our heads in to have a look. Either way, it was some of the most valuable – and fun – research we ever did.

If you get stuck on what to serve in your coffee house, and none of the above ideas strike a chord with you, then take a vacation, get out of your town, visit a good food city, and soak up some inspiration. It will be well worth it.

4.3 The Oyster: Creating an Atmosphere

Your retail environment is like an oyster. Why an oyster, you ask? Because an oyster is its own private world, protected from the outside by its shell. It is also a living thing, changing to suit the environment. The oyster in a retail setting is the environment you create for your customers. As if you were putting on a play, you want the stage to have a certain atmosphere to get the audience into the mood.

Every business – especially a coffee house – has an oyster. Some oysters happen as a result of a shop's environment and architecture; some happen out of the owner's ignorance; and some are created deliberately.

Take, for example, a café in a small town in Italy. Inside: The walls are weathered and covered with old photographs, the floor tiles are old and chipped – but clean – floor tiles, and there are open bottles of mineral water on tables with fresh flowers and clean linen tablecloths. Outside: The fragrance of olive trees is in the air, and the sun is beaming through imperfect panes of old glass windows.

This oyster was created over time; it is what it is with the help of geography and culture. But it has a definitive character about it that happened deliberately. In Italy, you are just as likely to find a business with no art, white walls, fluorescent lights humming, chipped cheap furniture, and unshaven employees.

In the United States, you can go into a Pottery Barn store and find furniture displayed in settings right out of *Architectural Digest* — with just the right lighting, contemporary music, and props like old books and art to give the feeling of what a home could be like with that type of furniture. In other words, as soon as you walk into a Pottery Barn, you walk into their world, which, in effect, is a fantasy world — a fantasy that you would like to be a part of.

On the other hand, you could walk into a real estate office with gray carpet, white walls without any art, fluorescent lights, agents dressed any way they want, and no music, just the hushed sound of people typing or talking on the phone. Sounds familiar, doesn't it? But what if you walked into a real estate office and it looked like a Pottery Barn? Wouldn't you feel better about spending a huge amount of money for a house in this place than in a cold, bleak office?

In a coffee house, the oyster is everything! Café Greco in San Francisco has the feel of Italy, with marble-top tables, high ceilings, and large mirrors. Just across the Bay in Berkeley, the café at the French Hotel seems a bit disheveled, with used newspapers laying around, loud music, and students deep in discussion. What type of coffee house do you want to have? Here are some ideas:

- A hip, upscale place with warm colors, high-tech lighting, and good jazz playing softly in the background. Your clients would be the professional type who may be stopping in for a latte to go.

- A student hangout where the furniture is used and eclectic and maybe a little worn. There will probably be a bookshelf with used books for sale. The music will be more prominent. The staff doesn't wear uniforms, and the menu changes daily.

- A retro-metro feel with lots of stainless steel, mirrors, neon, and bright colors. The coffee house is tied to an all-night Laundromat.

As you can see, there is no one way that a coffee house has to look or feel. What you can accomplish is totally up to you. First you need to come up with the overall idea for your coffee house, and then start to put together its oyster. The oyster is made up of five elements:

- Lighting

- Music

- Temperature

- Cleanliness

- Stage-Setting

Each one is very important and is connected to the others. Also, each one constantly changes. To manage the oyster is not that difficult once you get the hang of it. Let's look at each element separately.

4.3.1 Lighting

I can't say enough about the importance of lighting. In so many businesses this is taken for granted, when with just a little imagination it can be a critical part of the way you present your coffee house to customers.

Avoid Too Much Fluorescent Lighting

There are no steadfast rules to lighting because there are so many types of businesses. Some businesses need lots of lighting that is on full blast. Other businesses, like restaurants and coffee houses, need lighting that is more subtle and adjustable.

Take Safeway (**www.safeway.com**), a grocery store chain. It's a good store, but it has an institutional feel to it. Bright fluorescent lights do a good job of making it easy to see products, but the problem with that type of lighting is that it is cold and gray, and it tends to make the products on the shelves look unappealing.

In contrast, look at an organic grocery store like Whole Foods Market (**www.wholefoods.com**). They also use fluorescent lights, but only as a fill-in. The majority of the lights are pendants with regular light bulbs. The lights make the store look like an old warehouse, but they give off a warmer glow which not only makes the products look more appealing (the way you would see them in your home) but also makes the people shopping look better. Remember, fluorescent lights not only make products look gray, but they don't help the color of people's skin either.

A coffee house doesn't need fluorescent lights at all, except perhaps in the back kitchen, out of the public view. For the rest of your café, pick lights that match the type of coffee house you intend to have. You might just use track lighting, recessed lights, pendant lights, or a combination of all three. The important thing, though, is to have the lights on a dimmer switch (an adjustable on/off switch). That way, you can adjust the lights according to the outside natural light.

The general rule of thumb is that when the sun is at its brightest, you should keep the lights on at their brightest to balance out the sunlight. But as the sun goes down, so do the lights, softening the effect. If the lights are not bright enough during the day to balance out the sun, then the space feels too dark. If the lights are too bright when the sun goes down, it makes the space feel too cold and empty. However, if it is too dark inside when the sun goes down, then it is hard to see and feels a little claustrophobic.

You can mark your dimmer switches for the day and night shifts, but remember that there is the in-between time when you need to adjust them in small increments. Also remember to adjust your lights slowly enough so the adjustment is imperceptible to the customer.

Use Creative Light Fixtures

Interesting light fixtures can say a lot about your coffee house, too. Using lights as a design element can make the retail space more fun and creative. If you don't see the type of lights you want, you can always invent your own by using your imagination and whatever materials you can scrounge up. Old coffee cans make great shades for pendant lights. These days, anything goes for light fixtures.

4.3.2 Music

Music is one of my favorite subjects in the oyster analogy. It can add so much to the coffee house environment without costing much at all. Everyone is used to music in shopping malls, restaurants, and elevators. But the vast majority of businesses do not use this proven tool. I don't know why, other than that it might not fit in with their business, or the business owner just doesn't think about it. In most coffee houses it is a must!

There are two key factors to keep in mind: the type of music you play and the volume you play it at.

What to Play

The type of music you choose depends largely on the type of coffee house you have. If it has a bookstore feel, you might choose classical. If you were next to a university, you might choose something more "alternative." This decision largely depends on your clientele.

For instance, your coffee house might have a business crowd for lunch and a college crowd for dinner. You definitely wouldn't want the same type of music for both of these groups. It is best to understand all of your customers and be able to customize your music selection in order to reach them.

But even here there are more variables. You may have a customer base of people in their late 30s or early 40s. It might be interesting to play music that is a little younger and more rebellious to appeal to the rebel inside this age group. Or what about the opposite? How about Frank Sinatra and Tony Bennett for a college hangout? Who's to say it wouldn't work? The idea is to have fun with your music selection to see how it affects the customers. Play around with it.

> **TIP:** Under certain conditions, the American Society of Composers, Authors and Publishers (ASCAP) requires restaurants and cafés to pay licensing fees for music. Depending on the music you play, you may be subject to these fees. Refer to section 7.3.1 to learn more.

How Loud to Play Your Music

The volume of the music you play depends on the ambient sound level of your coffee house. If it is early and there are only a few customers, you might want the music to be a little louder, which would help fill in the silent gaps, making the store feel less vacant. However, if the coffee house is hopping, you might not want to have any music at all or at least not have it up as loud. When there is too much activity, the extra music just makes the whole scene feel out of control.

Still, you rarely can set the volume level and just leave it. Depending on how the music is mixed, some songs just seem louder than others. Or there may be an intense guitar or horn solo. Experiment with the volume. Turn the volume all the way down and watch your customers. You can actually feel the discomfort level. People start speaking more quietly so they can't be overheard. By playing with the volume control, you will eventually find the right level for your coffee house.

4.3.3 Temperature

The correct air temperature equals comfort. It's that simple. The temperature inside your coffee house will fluctuate according to the outside temperature and how many people are in the seating area. It also has a psychological impact on your customers. For example, if it is snowing outside, boost the heat so that customers come in from the snow to a blast of warm air and the aroma of coffee, welcoming them into the comfort of your coffee house. Or, if it is sweltering outside and you have a good air conditioner, turn it up so customers get that blast of cool air, and you can almost see them relax.

In business, we sometimes tend to forget about the temperature of our establishments unless the heating or cooling unit is broken. We also are not good indicators of the temperature because we are usually running around doing things, which makes us feel a little warmer than a customer just coming in the door. One good thing we can do, though, is to watch our customers' body language. If customers feel cold in your coffee house, usually you can tell by the way they cross their arms or put their hands in their pockets. If it is too hot, you can see the perspiration on their foreheads.

4.3.4 Cleanliness

Why is cleanliness so important, aside from the obvious? When customers walk into your coffee house and everything is clean and neat, there is a sense of order about the place. Think of how you feel in your own home. If there are dirty dishes in the sink, the trash can in the bathroom is overflowing, the bed isn't made, and clothes are on the floor, you feel a little out of control. It's upsetting. When you take the time to do the dishes, empty the garbage, make the bed, hang up the clothes– heck, even vacuum and do the laundry – you feel like you're really on top of things. You can't deny that this is a good feeling.

When you walk into a small retail shop and the service counter is cluttered with paperwork, the counter person's lunch, and old coffee stains, it's not a pleasant feeling. However, a store that has a clean counter and looks like it's ready for business just puts you at ease. The following are some areas of particular importance for your coffee house.

The Parking Lot

The parking lot is the first area your customers see, and it will say a lot about your coffee house. Get rid of cigarette butts and trash. Pull weeds. Plant flowers if you can. It's not hard to keep this area clean.

The Front Door

Keeping the front door clean includes cleaning the glass and the floor on the outside and inside of the door. Especially keep the handles to the door clean. You don't know what's on a customer's hands when they use a handle.

The Restrooms

Clean restrooms say a lot about a business's organizational ability. It always gripes me to see large national chains have really polished retail areas and trashed bathrooms. Once a restroom is clean, it only takes a couple of minutes a day to keep it that way. Add a few small touches like flowers or a side table where a woman can place her purse while using the restroom, and you will make a lot of customers very happy.

Floors and Walls

Put floors and walls on a regular maintenance schedule. If your floors are the highly polished kind, they need to stay that way. Carpets need to be cleaned on a regular basis to avoid dark paths. Tile floors collect dirt in the grout seams. Walls suffer from stains and chips taken out while moving things around. Touch up the paint often and repaint when needed.

Light Fixtures

Light fixtures are natural collectors of dust and spiderwebs. Dust them at least once a week.

Display Cases

Display cases should be spotless. After all, you don't want to display filth! This means not only having clean glass but also having everything inside neat and organized. The cleanliness of your coffee house is a direct result of the successful implementation of your checklist and audit systems (discussed later in the guide). What you are giving your customers is sense and order in the crazy world that they will deal with once they leave your place.

4.3.5 Stage-Setting

Stage setting is the touchy-feely part of the oyster. It's what you are trying to tell your customer about you. Our homes, our clothes, and the cars we drive are all picked out because they portray to the rest of the world who we believe we are. I drive a sports car because I want people to think I'm exciting. I wear the latest fashions so I will look cool. It's the same in our coffee house.

Look at an Eddie Bauer store. They sell clothes. So what's with the old books and lamps and canoes? They are selling a lifestyle, kind of an Ernest Hemingway thing. It goes further, too. The nice rich wood interior, slow-moving ceiling fans (*Casablanca*), easy lighting, appropriate music — it's a whole atmosphere.

Decide what you want to say about your coffee house — not just what you want to sell. People make purchases based on feelings, not always on what they need. What kind of feeling are you trying to get across to your customer?

Once you know what kind of feel you're going for, you can use the tools previously mentioned to achieve it with the addition of props. Props can be anything. Eddie Bauer uses canoes. McDonald's uses a playground. Blockbuster Video uses TVs showing featured movies. If I had a pet shop, I'd use a lot of big fake plants and an old jeep in the middle of the store with working headlights and a humidifier hooked up to the exhaust. Starbucks uses comfy leather chairs and jazz to evoke a particular feeling. Once you know what your coffee house is about, then your imagination can really take off.

4.4 Customers

Think about all the points of contact you have with your customers. At first it might seem that there are only two — when customers order and when they get their cup of coffee. The truth, however, isn't so simple. Let's count them up:

1. Customer sees your ad or sign.

2. Customer walks to your door from parking lot or front sidewalk.

3. Customer opens the front door.

4. Customer is greeted by someone at the counter.

5. Customer places an order.

6. Customer gets a cup of coffee.

7. Customer sits at a table.

8. Customer uses the restroom.

9. Customer orders something else.

10. Customer leaves through the front door.

There can be more or less, depending on how you set up your place, but think of all the opportunities to impress or disappoint someone. Ask yourself these questions:

- What kind of impression does your ad or sign make?

- Is the parking lot clean, and are the sidewalks swept?

- Is the front door clean, and does it open easily (even if you are in a wheelchair)?

- Are you greeted as soon as you walk in?

- How does the counter look?

- Is the counter person friendly and wearing a uniform?

- Is the menu easy to read?

- Are the tables clean and the chairs pushed up to the table in place?

- How does the restroom look?

- If you want to order something else, is there an easy way to do this without having to go back in line?

- When you leave, does someone say goodbye and thank you for your business?

Walkthrough

One way to view your coffee house like a customer is to conduct a walkthrough of your business. Starting with the moment when you arrive, list all the points of contact you can foresee your customers having with your coffee house. Just like in a play, choreograph a scenario that you would ideally like to see happen with your customers' experience in your business. Write down any creative ideas you have on how that customer might be treated or what the customer might experience.

After you write down this perfect scene in your play, script it by using your checklists. You can put anything down, such as having the employees park in a special place to reserve the good spots for customers. They can sweep the front sidewalk and clean the front door before a shift starts. Every hour, employees can spot-check the restrooms to make sure they are picked up and the mirrors are clean. All the product labels should be facing out and lined up evenly on shelves. Someone needs to greet your customers and say goodbye to them, as well.

This is a fun exercise and can give you a customer's perspective. You also might try asking some of your friends to make suggestions. No doubt they will have a different perspective than you will.

4.4.1 Comment Cards

Very few businesses can continue without changing. It's part of nature that everything changes. It is also part of the human psyche to want routine.

Have you ever been in a business where you had to do something that didn't make sense, and when you asked about it, management responded with, "Well, that's how we've always done it"? There are two opposing things taking place here: the natural way things need to change and our need for routine. Routine will win out if we do not have systems in place to enable change. In business, that system revolves around customer feedback.

As our businesses mature and our need for routine kicks in, we develop bureaucracy, our systems for doing things. We force our employees to conform to it. Worse, we force our customers to conform as well! The bottom line is not to upset your customers. This can happen if your system stops making sense. Believe me, the customer will let you know.

The system that we are discussing here doesn't change, but the market, customer preferences, new trends, products, and new technologies all do change.

To utilize customer feedback, you first have to have avenues available to receive this information. There are many ways to harvest these customer ideas to help your coffee house. You may have even more ideas than the ones I have, but the following ideas will get you thinking in the right direction.

Customer comment cards are cheap to make, have been around for a long time, and they work! They provide easy access for the customer to reach you. There are several things you can do with a customer comment card that will make it more user-friendly for your customers and more useful for you.

Make Them Available

Put a stack of customer comment cards everywhere your customer goes. Be creative in where you put them, such as at the cash register, in the restrooms, in to-go containers, on the back of receipts, or on car windshields.

Do whatever you can to get them in front of the customer without annoying him. Your message to your customers will be that you really want their opinions.

Make Them Easily Returnable

I like designing the customer comment card like a postcard. On the front of the postcard, place a picture of your coffee house, an item you want to push, or a picture of you. On the back, have an area where customers can fill out their comments.

Like a postcard, have your address already printed on it. If the comments are negative, it is much easier for the customer to return the card from the safety of a mailbox instead of handing it to you.

It can be a big plus to get a post office permit so the customer can just pop the postcard in the mail without having to place a stamp on it. If you are interested in getting a permit number from the post office, all that is required is for you to fill out an application and pay a $150 annual fee. The post office will show you how to print your cards so that the permit number looks uniform and is located in the right place. In addition to the annual fee, the post office will charge you an additional ten cents per piece of mail on top of the regular postage.

Get Customers' Information

Start to build a database on your customers. Ask for their name, address, phone number, and e-mail address. You can use this information for all sorts of things, including store promotions and demographics research. These e-mail addresses are a vital piece of information, as e-mail is an excellent way to communicate with your customers. It's fast and inexpensive, and almost everyone has it. And while some people may be reluctant to give you their personal information, it doesn't hurt to ask.

Answer Everyone

Every time you get a customer comment card, answer it that day. If you get a bunch, have each manager answer those they receive on their shift before they leave for the day.

Make up a postcard specifically for responding to positive comments. A simple note stating, "Thanks for the comments!" will suffice. The customer will get it back almost the next day and think, "Wow, these people are paying attention!"

If the customer gives you an e-mail address, add it to your customer database and send them a quick e-mail message as soon as possible. Speed is everything. If the customer has a reply sitting on their computer by the time they get home from having coffee at your place, they'll be so impressed that they will tell all their friends.

Negative comments should be handled differently. Send a handwritten or typed letter of apology as soon as possible. This should be followed up by a phone call. Tell the customer what steps you are taking to make sure that whatever happened to anger or annoy them won't happen again. You may want to offer a gift certificate or something similar to entice the customer to come back to your place. Remember, it costs less to keep customers than it costs to attract new ones.

Save Comment Cards for Your Manager Meeting

We'll talk about manager meetings a little later, but for now, don't throw away those cards as soon as you answer them. You will want to go over them at your manager meeting. The cards don't do any good unless you react to them. So use the information you receive. Your customers love to be heard, and this is how you let them know you're listening.

4.4.2 Frequent Customer Cards

Giving good customers a discount for repeat business is nothing new. It's a great way to build up business and take care of your loyal customers. With the advent of computer register systems that track purchases, it has never been easier to do this.

Have your customers apply for a frequent customer card. Almost any kind of card can have a bar code on the back that can be read by the computer each time the customer comes in for coffee. Give your customers a short application to fill out with as much or as little information as you want. My personal feeling is that in this day and age, it is best to just ask for a name, phone number, address, and e-mail. It is too much of an invasion of privacy to ask about people's age, how many kids they have, or what their income bracket is.

Once a customer is in the system, they can show their card when paying. It gets scanned in, and those sales are credited to that customer. You can then send out coupons or gift certificates when the customer reaches a certain amount in dollar sales. You decide what promotion you want to give. Just be sure to let the customer know what's in it for them!

If you are not into high-tech, there is always the punch card. Have cards printed up that customers can have punched every time they purchase something from you. Once their card has been punched a certain number of times, they are eligible for a discount or a free cup of coffee.

With either system, you are entering into a partnership with customers. If they keep returning, you reward their loyalty. It's definitely a win/win situation. The bonus is that, if your cash register can track such information, you can keep track of what your customers prefer, when they shop and how often. This is good direct feedback. (See section 3.3.1 to learn more about cash register options.)

4.4.3 Get to Know Your Customers

You still can't beat just having a conversation with a customer. Customers love to meet the person in charge because it makes them feel that they matter. Everyone has his own ideas about how you should run your business. These opinions are not always wrong.

Your customers have a unique perspective about your business that you could never have. You are too attached and know the business too intimately. On the other hand, your customers look at your business with fresh eyes. In many cases, they see it like a one-time visitor, so their point of view is completely fresh. Or, they compare their experience with experiences they've had with your competitors. So when they speak, you ought to listen.

5. Opening Your Coffee House

5.1 Pre-Opening Schedule

It is wise to open on a Monday, which is a slower day. This will give you and your employees a little adjustment time. However, the process of opening will actually begin on a Saturday, nine days before your official opening day.

Saturday

Have a meeting with all new employees to discuss the schedule of events for opening. This will include training and the times that different people will arrive for their specific training sessions. Make the meeting upbeat, and be well prepared. Definitely have coffee made and something for everyone to eat. Introduce yourself and any other managers and explain what the coffee house is all about.

If the group is small enough, have new employees introduce themselves as well. Keep the meeting short. No need to get long-winded about finally achieving your dream. Once everyone has their schedules, thank them for coming and tell them you will see them on Monday.

Sunday

This will be the quiet before the storm. You may want to have a couple of people from the Saturday meeting do a final cleaning, put away stock, decorate, or do other last minute chores. However, try to get out of there at a reasonable hour. Go home and rest up for the coming week.

Monday

Don't have everyone come in at the same time. Have everyone divided up by job description and, if it is a large group, divided again into small groups. For example, if you have six counter people, have a group "A" consist of three people who come in at one time and a group "B" that comes in at another. That way, you can work with a smaller number of people, and it will be easier for everyone to stay involved.

Teach the counter people the proper way to make espresso drinks and coffee. Whoever supplies your coffee may come and do this for you. Also, go over how to greet people, cleaning techniques, the checklist system, and how the service system will work. Have them each take a turn on the register ringing up fictitious orders to build speed.

If they have cooking duties, you may want to have group "B" working in the kitchen while group "A" is working at the counter, and then switch them. If you have separate kitchen people, they also should be divided into groups.

Your goal by the end of the day will be for the groups to further divide and serve each other. Do this a few times, and at the end of the day, have a meeting with everyone to discuss how things went. It will be rough, I guarantee it. But you will learn valuable things about how to set up the coffee house. If the placement of certain pieces of equipment doesn't work, you can change it before you open to the public. Or, if the flow at the cash register causes a bottleneck you hadn't expected, you will have the opportunity to correct this also.

Tuesday

Use this day the same way you used Monday, although you may want to switch the times you work with the groups. Today your employees will have a better idea of what is going on, and you will find things to be much easier. The important part of the day, other than the repeating of the training, will be when everyone serves one another.

At the end of the day, have a quick meeting to discuss what went right and what still needs improvement. Your employees will probably see areas for improvement that you have not seen. Finally, ask your employees to have some of their friends or relatives come in for free coffee and food on Wednesday evening. Give specific times for people to come and limit the number of people coming.

Wednesday

Go through the same training protocols you established on Monday and Tuesday. Through repetition, you can pick out any early trouble spots in the system or in the employees.

Wednesday is a dress rehearsal day. Your goal is to serve people who have never been in before — the friends and relatives of your employees. Things may have been smooth the day before, but for some reason, as soon as your new customers come in, things will start to break down.

Don't be alarmed. This is how everyone learns. Your customers won't mind, as it didn't cost them anything. They will feel like they are a part of the business and will want to help. Following the pattern, finish this day with a meeting to discuss what went right and what didn't.

The next day gets a little more serious.

Thursday

The goal today is to start serving people who you don't know. Invite people from around your business community, those in offices or neighborhoods who may likely be your customers anyway. Go door to door, and hand out invitations with a specific time on it. Stagger these times so that everyone doesn't come at once. Of course, you should expect that people won't show up when you scheduled them to. Most likely, they will all come at once. (This is real life after all!)

Try to find people who will be enthusiastic about the coffee house, those who are leaders in their circle of friends. If you win them over, they will tell many more people than would shy people who keep to themselves.

Much of the training has been done during the past three days of repetitive duties. Treat this as a normal shift with employees coming in and going though their normal routines. Once you are set up, you just need all those people you invited to show up.

You should position yourself at the door to greet people. Explain that this is all for training and that you would appreciate any suggestions they may have to offer. Give them a customer comment card, and ask them to fill it out at the end of their visit and leave it on the table. Tell them how much you appreciate them coming to help train your crew.

You also need to be at the door to keep out all the other people who want to come in because they think you are open. If you want, you can let some of them in to turn up the volume on the training.

Once again, have a meeting at the end of the shift to go over the comment cards and discuss the day.

Friday

Today is just like Thursday. Do everything the same, only with the improvements you have made since the day before. You will want to mix up your employees so they get the most experience possible.

Your goal today, however, is a smooth shift. After a long week, things should start to feel pretty comfortable. The crew should have some confidence and know what they are doing. They won't be perfect at their jobs, as they have only been working for one week, but they will be better than they were on Monday. Hopefully your comment cards will reflect this.

Saturday

Have a party! Make a separate invitation for this. Throw a grand-opening celebration, and set times for it to begin — and especially for it to end. Decide what you want to serve, and have some of your employees there to help serve and clean up.

Invite all your family and friends, the construction crew, the bankers, lawyers, accountants, and especially all the neighbors and people who have been coming the nights before. Pack the place! Make it fun, and, above all, make it short.

Stay at the door to greet people and to keep out curious passersby. Let everyone know that you will be officially open for business on Monday, and ask people to come back! It is always a good idea to ask people for their business.

Sunday

Rest. Sleep in. Read the paper, then go in to work and take a moment to enjoy the quiet. You are about to open, and you are sitting in your coffee house. You can use this day to make sure you have everything ready for your first day of business. Do what you need to do, then get out of there and enjoy a quiet day with family or friends or just keep to yourself and go to bed early.

Over the past week, you have spent a great deal of money on inventory and on wages. However, you may have noticed that I didn't suggest you take out any ads in newspapers or radio. If I did, you would have spent at least a couple of thousand dollars.

This week you spent a few thousand dollars, but you gained far more. Not only have you trained your employees well, but you also engaged a lot of potential customers, fed them, and made them feel that they are a part of your business. This, in effect, makes them goodwill ambassadors in the community. This is how word-of-mouth spreads. All the experts say this is the best form of advertising.

The bonus to opening this way is that your employees also receive the best kind of training because they had a chance to make a lot of coffee for real customers. You are now ready to start your coffee house with a well-trained staff and a good core customer base. Not a bad start. Now it's time to open!

5.2 Marketing

As I mentioned, word of mouth is the best kind of advertising. There are many ways to increase the chances of people passing along the good word and coming into your coffee house.

Let's face it — unless you are Starbucks, you probably don't have much in the way of an advertising budget. Don't worry: Some of the best marketing is done on the cheap and fits more with the atmosphere of a coffee house anyway.

Remember: Money follows imagination; imagination doesn't follow money. So not having buckets of cash is no hindrance to effective marketing. Here are some basics for marketing your coffee house the grassroots way.

5.2.1 Getting Bodies Through the Door

The number one goal of your business is to keep the customers you have and attract new ones. If you are doing a good job at keeping customers, they will tell others, who will in turn become new customers. If you are doing positive things to attract new customers, this will also keep it interesting so that your loyal customers keep coming back. Besides coffee, what are the other reasons people choose to go to a coffee house? Sometimes it is the coffee house atmosphere that your customers are after. Just as important, sometimes it is the community feeling that attracts customers to coffee houses.

Things that you can do to promote that community feeling will only add to the attractiveness of your business. These can be simple things, such as creating a community bulletin board where customers can post messages, or inviting a guest speaker to talk on some topic that is of current importance, like a bond issue or school board elections.

5.2.2 Live Music

A coffee house is the perfect venue for live performance. There is local talent in almost every town. Putting a sign by your cash register that you are looking for entertainers will bring them out of the woodwork. But an even better idea is to do a press release and let the local paper spread the word. (See section 5.2.4 for tips on writing press releases.)

You will need a corner of your dining room that is separate from the regular seating that can be converted for a live music performance. It is a good idea to have this area be mobile so that you can put this small stage away when you are not using it. You will also want some sort of lighting. It can be as simple as cheap spotlights you buy at the local hardware store, or you can spring for more professional – and more expensive – lighting. You may also choose to install a sound system so that musicians do not have to haul their own gear in every time they play.

If you want larger acts, you will of course need a much larger stage with more sophisticated equipment. But for now, let's assume that the Dixie Chicks will not be playing at your coffee house.

There are different ways in which to pay musicians. If you are planning a little larger act for a one-night show, you can charge a fee at the door. The fee can cover 100 percent of the cost of the entertainment, and if it is well attended, there may be some money left over for the coffee house as well. Or, you can have a guarantee for the band, so if the money received from the door isn't enough, you will agree to cough up the difference.

Being cheap myself, I like it when the musician plays for tips. The reason for my cheapness is some simple math. To do the math, just take the expenditure and divide by your net profit. If you pay a small bluegrass group $100 for an evening's performance, and you usually show a net profit of 10 percent, then you will have to do an extra $1,000 in sales just to pay for the band! If you net 5 percent, then the number jumps to $2,000. Depending on your choice of entertainment, you can accomplish these sales figures, but it is rare. So my advice is to bring in local talent and let them play for tips or a cut of the cover charge.

5.2.3 Donate

Good grassroots marketing always includes getting involved with local charities and other fundraisers. It is cheap and effective, and it helps worthwhile organizations raise money — which is a good thing. In addition, people that attend those functions are usually in the upper income brackets and are more likely to be your customers. It also associates your coffee house with the community and the ongoing well-being of your town.

At the brewery I used to run in Western Colorado, we donated beer to just about anyone who asked for it. If a group of volunteers was building a trail in the National Monument and our beer was served at their barbeque, then those volunteers would have associated our brewery with their cause.

In addition to having a sign with our brewery's name on it at the function, we usually got mentioned in any printed material the group sent out in return for our donation. When people are at a fundraiser, they usually feel pretty positive about what they are doing. If they were drinking a glass of our beer, well, you get the idea.

There are many ways to donate from your coffee house:

- A gift certificate for coffee

- A pound of coffee to be auctioned off

- Show up to the function and pour your coffee for free

- Volunteer your coffee house to host a fundraiser

- Give away cards good for a free cup of coffee

- Provide coffee to your local public radio station during their fund drive

- Sponsor a bowling league or a softball team

If you get the local paper, you can see what is going on in your community and contact the organizations that are trying to raise money. You may be surprised to find how many opportunities there are.

Donating product is more cost-effective than purchasing ad space. If you give away 100 cups of coffee that you normally sell for $1.50 each, that has a value to the charity of $150. However, your cost for the coffee will only run about $20. Second, instead of mass marketing your coffee, you have a target audience. People are more likely to actually try your coffee, whereas they may or may not pay attention to a radio spot.

If you want to market your coffee house without spending a whole lot of money, using it as a place to host fundraisers is about the most effective way to do it. It is one thing that you can do right away without huge budgets or planning. Just open the paper, make a phone call, and give it away. It will come back tenfold.

5.2.4 Press Releases

The news media is always looking for something to fill in the space between the ads, and it's not that easy. If you have something that is newsworthy, chances are it may be of interest to your local newspaper, radio, or television station. Best of all, it is free.

One of the best and most important press releases you can write is one announcing that you're opening for business. Other events can include special entertainment or guest speakers you are having at your coffee house, fundraisers you are doing, or new products you are introducing. If you are expanding, this makes a good press release for the business section of the paper. If you do a showing of local art, then you might want to do a press release for the paper's arts and entertainment section.

Your press release should be written so that it could be published "as is." Read the section of the paper where you would like to be published and use a similar writing style for your own news release. Below are some tips for writing a press release. Additional suggestions for writing a press release are available at **www. xpresspress.com/ PRnotes.html**.

- Make sure the press release is newsworthy. For example, you could write about an upcoming event you'll be participating in.

- Give your press release a strong lead paragraph that answers the six main questions: who, what, where, when, why, and how.

- Include factual information about yourself and your coffee house. Remember: A press release should read like a news story, not an advertisement.

- Keep it short. Aim for a maximum of 500 words.

- Include your contact information at the end of the press release so that reporters and readers can reach you.

Sample Press Release

FOR IMMEDIATE RELEASE

Contact: Mike Bigliano, Mike's House of Big Java
Phone: (555) 567-1234
Fax: (555) 567-4321
E-mail: mike@mikesbigjava.com

Mike's House of Big Java Starts Free Bicycle Program

Ashland, Oregon—Mike Bigliano, owner of Mike's House of Big Java, a local Ashland coffee house, announced Friday that the shop will start a free bicycle program that will provide free transportation to local residents.

The program, called Mike's Bikes, will start with 20 bicycles painted black and set out in different parts of town. The idea behind the program is that residents in need of a bike will be able to use the bicycle for the day and either return it to the place where they picked it up or to any other Mike's Bikes parking spot scattered around Ashland.

Says Bigliano: "Most of our customers arrive at our coffee house on a bike. We wanted to do something for our community as a thank-you, so we thought, Why not buy a bunch of bikes and just put them out there for people to use when they need them?"

Sarah Bigliano, Mike's partner, agrees. "Mike has a big heart, but it is not as simple as just putting a bunch of bikes out there," she explains. "First we buy used bikes or get them donated. Then we go through them to make sure they are mechanically sound and safe. Next we put baskets on the front of them so people can carry items on the bikes. We also have to be prepared to keep the bikes fixed, and we have organized a group of volunteers to work on bikes one Sunday a month. We're pretty excited about this".

Some of the considerations Mike and Sarah Bigliano had to deal with were the possibility that bikes would be stolen. "We are prepared for up to a 50% loss," says Bigliano. "We will continuously be getting more bikes until we saturate the town with free ones." Mike Bigliano also had to negotiate with other businesses to put bike racks in front of their stores where the bikes could be kept. "So far, the response has been terrific," adds Sarah Bigliano.

If you would like to donate a bike or need any additional information, please call Mike Bigliano at (555) 567-1234. Mike's House of Big Java is a 10-year-old coffee house that provides premium coffees from around the world by the cup or by the pound.

5.2.5 Free Coffee

When we had our wood oven pizza restaurants, our advertising budget was so small that all we could afford to do was give away a lot of pizza. But that seemed to do the trick.

Print up some business cards or coupons that say, "Good for one free coffee drink." Make sure the coupon also has:

- The name of your coffee house

- Your address

- Your phone number

- A map showing where your coffee house is located

- A place where you can sign the coupon to show that it has been redeemed

Always keep these with you to give out wherever you are. Hand them out with the tip at restaurants. Give one to the clerk at the grocery store. Walk through office buildings and give them away. Go to hotels and give them to the people at the front desk. It is a personal way to get people into your coffee house.

Most people will use the card, and your cost will probably be less than 50 cents apiece, depending on whether they get a cup of coffee or a specialty coffee drink. (If you want, you can specify a price limit on the card so you don't end up giving away the most expensive drink on the menu.) That's pretty cheap advertising. The next time they come in, they will probably bring someone in with them.

> **NOTE:** If you choose to pass out these cards, be sensitive that you don't appear as though you are soliciting. Some businesses will have signs on their door prohibiting this activity, and you should respect that. The idea of giving these cards out should be a positive gesture, not a simple sales call. There is a difference, and you will have to use your own common sense to know which is which.

Marketing your coffee house is just an exercise in imagination. No matter how busy you become, you always want to be marketing your business to keep it in the minds of your existing customers and to bring in new ones.

5.2.6 The Internet

Just about everybody has Internet access, yet many business owners do not utilize this simple tool. But it is currently one of the most direct ways to let your customers speak to you without being right in front of them.

People like the Internet because it provides privacy. They are more likely to give you feedback about what they liked or didn't like about their visit to your coffee house if they can do it from their own home. It is hard to tell you to your face that your coffee stinks. It is so much easier to pop over to your website and send you a note that says, "Great service, but your coffee stinks!"

Every business should have a website for the simple reason that it is a great way for people to contact you. Besides the obvious benefits of promoting your business by linking your page to search engines, a website offers a unique form of customer feedback.

Developing a Website

If you are already experienced at creating Web pages, or if you learn quickly, you can design your website yourself using a program such as Microsoft's Front Page or Netscape Composer (free with the Netscape Browser). Otherwise, it's a good idea to hire a professional Web designer through word of mouth or by finding one in the Yellow Pages. Of course, you should visit sample sites the designer has created before hiring her.

You may be able to put up a free Web page through your Internet Service Provider (the company that gives you access to the Internet). To present a professional image and make your Web address easier for clients to remember, consider getting your own domain name, such as **www.NameOfYourCoffeeHouse.com**. More and more people are beginning to assume that they can just add the "www" prefix in front of the name of your business and find it online.

There are a number of sites where you can search for and register a domain name. The most popular of these is GoDaddy (**www.godaddy. com**).

Once you register your domain name, you will need to find a place to host your site. GoDaddy provides that service, and your Internet Service Provider may provide it also. You can find a wide variety of other companies that provide hosting services by doing an online search. (Do not use a free Web hosting service unless you don't mind having your customers see pop-up ads for products like spy cameras!)

Promoting Your Website

Once you have a Web address, put that address everywhere you can. Some suggestions include:

- On printed material

- On vehicles

- On merchandise like hats, T-shirts, and coffee mugs

- Seen through advertising such as TV, radio, and print

- On your customer comment cards

- In restrooms

- Everywhere you can!

It is like fishing. You need to cast your lines into many different waters if you are going to be successful. Customer comments are gold nuggets of information. They provide feedback to let you know if you are going to stay in business. It is that important!

6. Managing Your Coffee House

6.1 The Business System

Why do some businesses succeed and others fail? Look around your town at the businesses that do well and the ones that are struggling. Chances are that some of the struggling businesses are actually quite good and the ones that seem so busy are somewhat mediocre.

A perfect example that has been used by many is McDonald's. There is probably at least one in your town. There may also be a small hamburger joint in the same town. It is not unusual for the hamburgers in the mom-and-pop burger restaurant to be better than the thin burgers that have been under a warming lamp at McDonald's. But McDonald's is packed and the mom-and-pop is just getting by.

It is true that McDonald's has national advertising, but it has something even more important — a business system. The mom-and-pop burger joint probably doesn't have one. There, the quality of the product depends largely on the moods of the owners and managers on any particular day. If they are happy, they greet the customers with a smile and prepare the food efficiently. If they are in a bad mood – because someone didn't show up to work, they forgot to order supplies, or a piece of equipment broke down – the service suffers.

6.1.1 Your Operation System

An operation system is at the guts of a successful business. It is the behind-the-scenes structure that keeps the business operating in a smooth and efficient manner. It deals with all of the details in running a business, from training employees, to maintaining equipment, to marketing, to how the cash is managed. For instance, when you go into a Home Depot, employees go out of their way to ask you if you need any assistance. If you ask where an item is, they not only tell you but also walk you to the location. That's their system.

When you order from McDonald's, they always ask you if you want fries with your order. That's their system. When I bought a Honda from a dealership, I continually received reminders for tune-ups and special deals. I didn't receive those cards because some excellent employee remembered to send me one. They had a business operating system that made it happen.

To be successful in your coffee house, you need a good system. You have an advantage over Starbucks because you are a local owner. However, Starbucks has an advantage over you because they have an excellent business system.

To give you a better chance against the chain coffee houses, this next section will give you a system for operating your coffee house and help you achieve financial success.

In order to do this, the operating system needs to:

- Provide consistency in product, service, and atmosphere

- Allow the business to change rapidly with economic and social conditions

- Assure that the business is making money

Managing cash flow will provide the capital needed not only for wages and equipment but also for personal financial growth. (I'm assuming that you want to make money out of this business as well as have fun in it!)

We'll start with the basics of how to keep the business consistent. This is real nuts and bolts stuff that covers employee training, day-to-day operations, and how the daily books are done. We'll finish up with a system that will allow for the changes that are necessary in order for your business to grow, but in a framework that keeps it consistent. This way, your customers have the security in knowing what to expect when they come into your coffee house. That, as far as I can figure it out, is why people keep coming back to McDonald's.

6.2 Hiring Your Staff

6.2.1 Identify Coffee House Positions

First of all, you need to identify all the positions in your business. This is not how many employees you have, but what the actual positions are. Employees move around in positions, but the positions themselves stay pretty much the same. If you have someone who is the principal espresso maker, then that is a position. Someone whose main focus is the cash register would also be considered a separate position. The same goes for cooks and dishwashers, if you have them.

As your business grows, you may add positions such as assistant manager, bus person, and so on. Many of your employees will learn more than one position. It's important to make up the checklists for the positions and not for the individuals in those positions.

6.2.2 Advertising

Don't wait until the last minute to let the public know you will be hiring. While under construction, have a large sign in the window explaining your coffee house to the public. This sign should also let potential employees know how they can get in touch with you for interviews. During the early days of construction, just take their names and phone numbers and get in touch with them as the opening date approaches.

When you actually start to advertise for help, only accept applications at specific times, say 3:00 p.m. to 4:00 p.m. That way you will not be constantly interrupted with applicants while you are in the final days of construction. By setting aside specific times, you can give your undivided attention to the prospective employee.

6.2.3 Non-Negotiable Sheet

A great way to start with a possible employee is to give them a non-negotiable sheet before they fill out an application. The non-negotiable sheet explains up front all the things about your business that you will hold the line on.

It could include such things as hair that is only of a natural color (not green or blue), no pierced eyebrows, or no visible tattoos. It is whatever is important enough to you that you will not negotiate about it with the new employee. Then, if the employee agrees with the items listed on this paper, they can fill out an application.

This is not legally binding, but it is a good way to let this person know how you feel about certain things. You are being up-front and honest by informing the potential employee how you feel about certain things in your business. Isn't that a better way to begin a relationship?

Here are some things to consider putting on your non-negotiable sheet:

- No visible tattoos

- Hair of a natural color only

- Body piercing limited to ears only

- Willingness to work on holidays

- Full beard or mustache, or clean shaven. Nothing in between.

6.2.4 Interviews

General Questions

When you set up your interview, have a list of questions prepared in advance. This will keep the process consistent between applicants. You can always add questions that pop up based on their answers as you go along.

A good first question to ask is why they applied with you in the first place. If they have a sense of humor, they will use it at this point. If they are sincere, they will tell you the truth. If they aren't sure, they will shrug their shoulders and say they don't know. Here are some other questions to ask:

- What is the ideal schedule you would like to work?

- When can you absolutely not work?

- Do you have any special needs or disabilities?

Specific Questions

Next, delve into an area that will give you a little insight into what the person is like and how they may fit into your coffee house:

- What sort of experience do you have that you feel qualifies you for this job?

- Tell me about your last job and why you left.

- What was the best job you ever had? The one you had the most fun in?

- Who was your best boss and what made him or her so great?

- If I talked to someone who worked with you, what would they say about your work habits?

- Do you have any ambitions in this business? If not, what would be your perfect job?

After the interview, thank the candidate for their time and tell them that you will call them either for a second interview or to let them know that the job has already been filled. Either way, you will let them know.

Second Interview

If you feel the person has good potential, schedule them for a second interview with another manager or your partners. It is a good idea to get another opinion about a potential employee. But if there is no one else, then you will need to do the second interview yourself.

There should be a cool-down period between the first and second interview to gain perspective on the potential employee. In the second interview, you can ask the person specific questions regarding the position and give them more information as well. This is usually a shorter interview. Finally, tell them that you will call them with your decision and that if it works out, you hope that they will choose to join your team.

TIP: Write your initial impressions of an employee on a sticky note and attach it to their application. It will help you re-member the person later when you are interviewing the applicants. The notes can be thrown away later, so they do not become part of the employee's permanent files.

Check References

In between the first and second interview, you will want to check the employee's references. It is amazing how rarely businesses look at references. You could argue that many employees won't list bad references, but in my experience, that isn't usually the case.

We once had a manager who took off to Hawaii with the weekend deposit. He was eventually caught and the insurance company made a deal with him not to prosecute if he returned the money. About two years later, we received a call from an employer checking on his references. We couldn't believe it; he actually put us down as a reference! We couldn't tell the person checking references that the guy was a thief, but we could say that he was not eligible for rehire.

If you check references, you will save yourself some headaches and a lot of money used for training. The key question, therefore, would be to ask if the employee was eligible for rehire or not. A former employer may not tell you all the dirt on an employee for liability reasons, but they can let you know if they would hire that person again.

Reference Questions

Here are some other good questions to ask when checking references:

- How long did this person work for you? (This establishes the accuracy of their application.)

- How well did they get along with everyone? (Team skills.)

- Did they take direction well? (Code words for "Did she do her job?")

- Could they work independently? (Or did they sit around waiting to be told what to do next?)

- How did they handle stressful situations? (This is important, especially if you are busy.)

If the references make you feel comfortable about the person, call to let them know that they have the job and to come in and fill out the paperwork. If it doesn't work out, call the candidate anyway and tell them that the job has been filled but that you appreciate them applying and that you wish them luck. Remember, you still want the person as a customer and want no ill feelings between you. This small amount of work will pay dividends in the future.

6.2.5 New Employee Paperwork

Now that you've hired this employee, there is a certain amount of paperwork they must fill out. Start an employee file with the employee's name on the front and all the paperwork that the government requires you to have inside the file. In the United States, this will be a W-4 (Employee Withholding Allowance Certificate) and an I-9 (Employment Eligibility Verification Form).

For more information, check online with the IRS (**www.irs.gov**) and Canada Revenue Agency (**www.cra-arc.gc.ca**).

Employee Manual

Besides tax forms, the most important document you can give a new employee is the employee manual. This is a simple document that explains the basic details of your coffee house and the guidelines for working there.

The employee manual should include:

An Introduction

Begin with a couple of paragraphs congratulating the new employee for joining your coffee house team. Let the person know that they are responsible for reading and understanding all the information inside the manual.

Company History

Tell the reader how the coffee house began, and tell them a little bit about yourself. It really helps new employees feel like they are a part of the coffee house if they know some of the intimate details about how it all began.

Policy and Procedures

Here you will cover the following specifics that the new employee should know about:

- Address and phone number

- Phone usage

- Pay periods

- Employee uniforms

- Breaks

- Calling in sick

- Schedules

- Employee parking

- Hours of operation

- Holidays

- Employee benefits

- Discipline procedures (what it takes to get fired)

- What to do in case of injury

- Care and use of the equipment

You may have some other things you want to include that are specific to your operation.

Signed Acknowledgement

The last page in the employee manual should be an acknowledgement page for the employee to sign. It is not legally binding, but it does impress upon the new employee that you are serious about the information in the manual and that you expect them to know the material. It can be as simple as a line that says, "I, [employee's name], have read the employee manual and agree to the contents therein," followed by a blank line for the employee to sign and date.

Once the employee signs and dates the last page, tear it off and keep it in their file. Let the person keep the manual for future reference. With a signed copy of the agreement, it is harder for the employee to say, "Well, no one ever told me that" in the future. This simple tool will save you a lot of headaches.

Other Paperwork

In addition to the employee manual, you will want to give the employee a job description, a training checklist, and any other information they will need.

Blank folders should be made up ahead of time so that you're ready to go when you hire a new employee. Write the employee's name on the folder, and put it into your employee files. Employee evaluations and raise information can be added later for future reference.

Once you have the employee in front of you, take the time to go through the paperwork with them. Do this now — you won't have time later when things get rolling. If you take the time up-front, you can be assured that the employee knows what's expected of them.

Also be sure to go over their job description, and answer any questions they have. When you are done, take the new employee on a tour, and explain where everything is, including parking, the employee break area, and other details.

This process should take about 15 to 30 minutes, and it is time well spent. First impressions mean something, and when the new employee sees you take such a keen interest right from the beginning, they will subconsciously know that their job is very important to you. Your enthusiasm for the coffee house will come through, and it will be infectious. The person may even catch the fever for your dream! In addition, they will not be able to use the excuse that they were not informed.

6.3 Training Employees

Most businesses tout their great training programs. Some develop videos for new employees to watch, while others send employees to training schools. However, many do not follow up on their lofty schemes. If there isn't a thorough follow-through, even what I suggest here doesn't amount to a hill of beans. The basic system is pretty simple.

6.3.1 Employee Training Ideas

Sue Smith comes to work at the coffee house as a barista. She has already filled out her paperwork, gotten a tour, and been issued a uniform. She is assigned a trainer on her first day on the job. Her trainer is someone who knows the job well and is paid a small premium to train new employees. The trainer receives a training checklist from the manager and takes a few minutes to go over some of the simple things on the list with Sue. These would be items like where to park, the phone number, hours of operation, and what credit cards are accepted.

Next, the two of them spend the rest of the day performing the job but using the training checklist as a reference point along the way. At the end of the shift, the trainer goes back through the checklist and quizzes Sue on all of the items covered. The trainer explains to Sue that she will not be able to work on her own until she can pass a small written test covering the items on the training checklist.

Sue is scheduled to train for two more days; on each day she will be with a trainer (perhaps not the same person) and trained on the same checklist. By going over the same list everyday and being quizzed on the same material, it is more likely that Sue will absorb it. At the end of her third day, she sits down and takes a short written test. If she passes, she is on the schedule by herself. If she fails, she gets another day of training, followed by another test.

It takes time and money to do this properly, and you can't be short-sighted about it. A poorly trained employee can cost your business a lot more than it costs to train them. The turnover rate among poorly trained employees is higher, which means you'll end up constantly having to train new employees when your time could be better spent elsewhere.

Sample Training Checklist #1

Barista and Register Person — 3 Days

_____ Tour of coffee house
_____ Harassment policy
_____ Uniform policy
_____ How to clock in
_____ Employee meal policy
_____ Schedules, schedule requests, and pay periods
_____ Breaks and break area
_____ Parking
_____ Hours of operation
_____ Phone number, address, and phone usage policy
_____ Personal appearance and conduct in front of customers
_____ Starting times and where they are posted
_____ Teamwork policy, helping when not busy
_____ Economy of steps, never be empty-handed
_____ Greeting regulars and new customers (learn names)
_____ How to answer the phone
_____ How to handle to-go orders
_____ How coffee is produced and roasted
_____ How coffee is ground
_____ How coffee is brewed
_____ How to make a perfect espresso
_____ Coffee drink recipes
_____ Cleaning of espresso machine and coffee brewer
_____ How to work the register
_____ How to work the credit card machine
_____ Clean-as-you-go policy
_____ Sidework checklists
_____ Manager checkouts

Trainer: _____

Employee: _____

Date: _____

Sample Training Checklist #2

Kitchen Person — 3 Days

_____ Tour of coffee house
_____ Harassment policy
_____ Uniform policy
_____ How to clock in
_____ Employee meal policy
_____ Schedules, schedule requests, and pay periods
_____ Breaks and break area
_____ Parking
_____ Hours of operation
_____ Phone number, address, and phone usage policy
_____ Personal appearance and conduct in front of customers
_____ Starting times and where they are posted
_____ Teamwork policy, helping when not busy
_____ Economy of steps, never be empty-handed
_____ Greeting regulars and new customers (learn names)
_____ How to answer the phone
_____ How to handle to-go orders
_____ Defrosting techniques
_____ Recipe book
_____ Prep lists
_____ Reading tickets
_____ FIFO (first in, first out) dating boxes and rotating inventory
_____ Operation of sandwich press
_____ Operation of slicer
_____ Operation of mixer
_____ How to take out the trash
_____ Care of equipment
_____ Sanitary methods for handling food
_____ Clean-as-you-go policy
_____ Sidework checklists
_____ Manager checkouts

Trainer: _____

Employee: _____

Date: _____

6.3.2 Solutions to Training Glitches

Glitches usually occur because a trainer is too busy to devote the proper amount of time to teaching the new employee. In this case, Sue stops training and just starts working. This is a bad thing; this is not training. One of the worst things you can do for your new employee, and consequently your business, is to have them work solo without the proper training. This is why it is imperative that the new employee is tested before they are allowed to work their first shift alone.

The test is only to let you know that the employee has a basic understanding of the position and the business. It will still take some time before they are good at their job. The test can be as short or as long as you like. It can be written or oral. I prefer written because you then have a record of what the employee knows about the job. It helps you avoid the "no one ever told me that" syndrome.

Testing is sort of a certification process. You don't want a cook filling in for a barista if they don't know the first thing about how to make a proper espresso. If the cook wants to be able to fill in for the barista on occasion, they need to first be trained and then tested in that position.

6.3.3 Red and Blue Employees

As you schedule employees, situations come up where an employee needs a day off, or someone calls in sick and you are required to fill that spot in a hurry. When this happens, the key to maintaining sanity is to fill in the position with a qualified employee who has been trained for it. You need an employee that will cause the least amount of disruption in service to the customer and overall operation of the coffee house.

The way to identify these employees is by a simple system of using colors on the schedule for their names. I like blue and red because they are easy to see on a white piece of paper.

Red vs. Blue

Red Employees

If an employee is adequately trained for a position, they will have been tested and will therefore have a basic knowledge of the job. If the employee knows how to do one job, they are a "red" employee.

Blue Employees

Over time, some employees become so good at their jobs that they learn other positions and get tested to certify that they can work those other jobs properly as well. When a person knows how to do more than one job, they become a "blue" employee.

Using the System

When you make your schedules, write the names of the skilled employees – the ones who can do more than one job – in blue. Write the names of the newer or less motivated employees in red. With a quick glance, you can look at the schedule and see who is available to cover any shift. You know that a blue employee can cover anything they've been trained for.

The employees will know the difference between red and blue employees. It ignites their natural competitive spirit. It's right there in front of them on the schedule sheet. Who wants to be a red employee?

Even if they say they don't care, they do. Of course, some of your employees will not have the natural talent to be a star. But if their heart is in it, they will become blue employees in time. It really does come down to heart as much as talent. After all, your customers recognize heart and sincerity as much as talent, and you should also.

When you make a schedule, always schedule at least one blue employee per shift if possible. That way you know that there will be at least one person who can help others if an emergency arises. Blue employees are more versatile. If someone calls in sick or doesn't show up at the last minute, you can do a quick shuffle and get things covered. This makes a great safety valve.

6.4 Employee Checklists

If you want something done consistently, you need a daily reminder. You need to follow a checklist just to remind you of all the small details that are essential to running your business.

A simple list of things to do on any given day is one of the most powerful business tools available to you. It doesn't have to be fancy. It can be hand printed on regular paper with your kid's crayons if you want. In fact, it is better not to beautifully laminate and frame your checklists. Your goal is not to be rigid with systems. The system should be able to change at the drop of a hat, depending on how your business changes, the time of year, or special occasions.

One of our first restaurants had almost 100 employees. What a headache! When we started, we used only bare-bones checklists, which revolved around opening and closing duties. As time went on, it became obvious that we needed to commit more detail to paper and try to spread the workload out among everyone from dishwashers to management.

We looked at larger restaurant chains and other businesses to see how they dealt with this issue. In addition to having some impressive training systems, they all had terrific checklists. This all seems obvious to me now, but back then it was revolutionary.

You need a checklist for each position in your business. These positions may have early and late shifts as well. If that is the case, then you will need to specify that on the top of the checklist. For example, if it is the morning shift, you might have the heading "A.M. Barista." This shift's checklist might concentrate more on opening duties such as stocking, sweeping, and setup. A closing checklist might be headed "P.M. Barista" and would have all the cleanup and restocking duties.

Find a good location to keep all the checklists, or have each checklist in the area where the positions tend to be located. However, do try to keep them in a place where your customers won't see them.

6.4.1 Where to Start

Now that you have decided how many checklists you need, what are you going to put on them?

The Perfect Employee

You could start by writing all the things that the particular position should do, but there's a loftier goal I have in mind. I suggest you start by asking yourself what the perfect employee would be like in this position.

For example, make a list of all the things you would like the day barista to do in a shift. Now picture the Supreme Barista of All Time in that position, and ask yourself, "What is it that would make that employee so great?" This simple method will add a new perspective to creating the checklist. This person may do more than the basic job description. They may be constantly picking up those small pieces of litter on the café's floor all the time. They might sweep outside once a shift, or come to work with a nice clean uniform. This perspective adds a different slant into making up simple checklists. It lets you see more possibilities and new ways to improve your business.

Inspiring Coffee Houses

One thing that will help to figure out what the perfect employee might do is to visit similar businesses that you admire, and watch what their employees do. Maybe you have an aunt in San Francisco, a brother in Chicago, or a cousin in Quebec that you could visit. See what great places are around and visit them. Watch how they dress, greet customers, and handle complaints. Look at the facility and notice how clean it is. I can't overemphasize this enough — look at great examples of coffee houses and get inspired!

The act of making your checklists around the perfect employee adds a whole new dimension to the way you think about your business. Not only are you tightening up all the loose ends, but you are also creating new ways in which you think about your business and the way it relates to your customers. This is big medicine for your business.

6.4.2 Daily Duties

You might want to put some reminders in each checklist, like "Say hello to every customer who walks in the door" or "Don't walk back to the kitchen empty-handed." The last thing on the list should be "Check out with a manager." The checklists don't mean very much if no one is doing them. By having each person check out with a manager at the end of their shift, the manager can make sure all the checklists are actually done.

Of course, in the "real world" there will be times when you can't check every employee out due to time constraints. In those instances, just go over their list later to see if they did their job properly. Whether they did or they didn't, let them know that you checked. It is important that no matter what, you check and that your employees know how consistent you are. This consistency will help develop trust in your employees. Many companies make big promises in their employee manual about this or that, but in reality, few follow through. Make this commitment, and you won't be disappointed.

6.4.3 Weekly Duties

In addition to the daily duties that an employee must perform, there are some things that only need to be done occasionally. These can be posted on the bottom of the checklists and divided by A.M. and P.M., so that each shift has extra work that can be done on any given day.

All the things that need attention in your business become more manageable when you spread them out over all of your employees. During each shift, someone is doing something above and beyond the daily things that need to happen to keep your coffee house going. You may even find that you have a hard time filling in all the slots of opportunity to get things done.

On each individual checklist, make room at the bottom of the sheet for a list of extra work to be done for each day of the week. Include every shift that there is in a day. Each employee will have one extra bit of sidework to do per shift. It's not a big deal and the employee can do this extra work as they have time during their shift.

What types of items are on this? It's totally up to you. Some ideas might include things like dusting the chairs in the dining room or wiping down the cove base (the little area where the floor meets the wall). These are things that don't have to be cleaned everyday, but need attention every week. By adding these things to your checklists, so many projects will be done consistently that you will see a drastic improvement in the way your business looks from the very first day.

Put this together with the regular checklist and your complete documents might look something like this:

Sample Barista Checklist

Opening

___ Set up counter
___ Make coffees
___ Wipe down tables and chairs
___ Write coffee specials on chalkboard
___ Count cash register
___ Clean glass on front door
___ Bring up clean cups and glasses from dish station
___ Set up espresso station
___ Pick up trash outside

Closing

___ Restock milk, coffee, condiments, and paper supplies
___ Wipe down counter area
___ Sweep and mop counter area floor
___ Empty trash
___ Clean coffee equipment
___ Check out with manager

Weekly

AM Mon   Dust display cabinets
PM Mon   Dust light fixtures

AM Tue   Bleach coffee cups
PM Tue   Empty salt, pepper, and sugar cruets; run through dishwasher

AM Wed   Clean glass matting behind counter
PM Wed   Wipe down walls of counter area

AM Thu   Dust all chairs
PM Thu   Dust pictures and mirrors

AM Fri   Wipe down all baseboards
PM Fri   Wipe down all table bases

AM Sat   Empty bulk coffee bins, clean, and refill
PM Sat   Empty, clean, and refill beverage cooler

AM Sun   Clean windows and doors
PM Sun   Open project — check with manager

Sample Register Checklist

Opening

_____ Fill salt and pepper shakers and sugars
_____ Check register and credit card paper
_____ Stock to-go items
_____ Clean cash register
_____ Clean all mirrors and pictures and straighten
_____ Dust merchandise and merchandise shelf
_____ Clean and organize community bulletin board
_____ Clean menus, and replace if needed
_____ Pick up trash outside

Closing

_____ Restock register and credit card machine paper
_____ Wipe down register area
_____ Sweep and mop dining area floor
_____ Help empty trash
_____ Bring up supplies from dish station
_____ Check out with manager

Weekly

AM Mon   Dust merchandise area
PM Mon   Clean counter trash cans

AM Tue   Hose down parking lot
PM Tue   With a broom, dust ceiling corners

AM Wed   Clean table tents
PM Wed   Empty, clean, and refill beverage cooler

AM Thu   Clean glass on all art
PM Thu   Dust pictures and mirrors

AM Fri   Clean under bar and tabletops
PM Fri   Take merchandise inventory

AM Sat   Take menus out of inserts and clean inserts
PM Sat   Clean and organize supply shelf

AM Sun   Clean behind coffee house
PM Sun   Open project — check with manager

Sample Kitchen Checklist

Opening

_____ Bring up mats and trash cans
_____ Set up cook station
_____ Prep food for day
_____ Put away and date food delivery
_____ Pre-prep sandwiches
_____ Fill pastry case with baked goods

Closing

_____ Change insert pans
_____ Cover all food items
_____ Wipe down counter area
_____ Sweep and mop counter area floor
_____ Empty trash
_____ Clean kitchen equipment
_____ Check out with manager

Weekly

AM Mon	Clean floor sinks with cleanser
PM Mon	Clean baseboards
AM Tue	Blow out compressor screens on refrigerators
PM Tue	Clean spice shelf
AM Wed	Empty sandwich prep table and clean
PM Wed	Wipe down walls of counter area
AM Thu	Clean out walk-in cooler
PM Thu	Clean kitchen windows
AM Fri	Hose out all trash cans
PM Fri	Clean floor sinks with cleanser
AM Sat	Clean hood screens
PM Sat	Dust lights in kitchen area
AM Sun	Clean hood
PM Sun	Open project — check with manager

6.4.4 Manager Checklist

The checklist for the manager is just as important, if not more important, than the one you make for each of your employees. It makes a difference when the manager can come to work in the morning, grab their list on a clipboard, and go through all the reminders of different tasks that need to be done on a daily basis.

Some can be as simple as a reminder to check the employee schedule to see who is coming in for the day. That can prevent a scheduling mistake where you end up being short a person. Other tasks can be things like putting the deposit together for the bank, picking the coffee specials for the day, or setting the lights and music before opening.

There are certain things you need on the list that provide a redundancy to the items on the employee lists. For example, the last item on the employee's list may be to get checked out by a manager, while the manager's list will have a reminder to check out the employees. This way, it is less likely that this important job will be forgotten.

You can also add things like a walkthrough inspection before you open to make sure the open sign is on, or that the flowers outside your front door are healthy, watered, and not full of cigarette butts.

> **NOTE:** This is a good place to mention that it is best to have an employee smoking and/or break area away from where your customers can see them. Smoking is looked upon as an unclean habit and can give a negative impression to your customers.

Conversing With Customers

Your manager's checklist should include talking to a given number of customers each shift. Ask them what they think of the coffee house. If they don't like it that much, ask them what they would do differently.

When they speak, look them in the eye — show them that you are interested. Don't look around the room at everything else that is going on, nodding your head as if you were listening.

Your customers will not only appreciate the fact that you want to know but will leave feeling that they too have a stake in your success. Also, be humble. Don't act like a big shot in front of your customers. People like to see the little guys succeed and the big ones shown their place.

It is true that when you talk to your customers face to face, they are less likely to tell you what is wrong. However, by taking the time to talk to them, they are less likely to go out of their way to trash your name to their friends, if they had a less than great experience. You have nothing to lose by simply taking the time to talk to your customers.

Here are some suggestions for things to go on your manager checklist:

Sample Manager Checklist

A.M.

_____ Check schedule
_____ Read logbook
_____ Count change bank
_____ Do deposit
_____ Check in deliveries
_____ Set lights and music
_____ Do preopening walkthrough
_____ Check GM book
_____ Talk to customers
_____ Monitor floor activities
_____ Check out employees
_____ Write in logbook
_____ Count A.M. cash drawer
_____ Meet with P.M. manager

P.M.

_____ Check schedule
_____ Check scoreboard (more on this later)
_____ Walkthrough
_____ Monitor floor activities
_____ Check out employees
_____ Ring out registers
_____ Run credit card machine
_____ Write in logbook
_____ Turn off all lights
_____ Make sure back door is locked
_____ Set alarm

6.5 Maintenance and Repairs

6.5.1 The General Maintenance (GM) Book

Some things do not need to be done on a daily or weekly basis. These reminders need to be tied more to a calendar than to the week. Perhaps these are things that need to be done every other week or once a month. This is where we use something called a General Maintenance (GM) book.

To make a GM book, you will need to get a three-ring binder and 31 tab dividers (one for each potential day of the month) from your local office supply store. In between each tab divider, put a piece of paper on which you will write all the reminders you need. This is usually just one piece of paper that you will write on in between the tabs. You don't have to do anything fancy, just write down things you will want to remember.

For example, you might have reminders to pay certain taxes that are due by a given date. Or, you may insert a reminder that on day 25 of the month, the Chamber of Commerce puts out its monthly calendar of upcoming conventions that could affect your business.

The GM book is also great for handling maintenance concerns. For instance, it is a good idea to clean the screens on the compressors on all your refrigeration equipment at least twice a month. This can save you a lot of cash by not having to replace a compressor that overheated because of dirty compressor screens.

Other things you may wish to put in the GM book include:

- Restocking office supplies

- Updating the website

- Making new blank employee paperwork files

- Contacting the local school district to check on school holidays

- Scheduling employee reviews

If you remember from the last section, one of the items on the sample manager's checklist was to check the GM book. The GM book won't do you any good unless you remember to pick it up every day and look at it. The manager's daily checklist reminds you to do that.

There may be days when the coffee house is hectic and you just can't get to the GM book. Other days, you may be swimming in free time and you can get a week's worth of GM book duties done. Nothing is set in stone. This is just a simple system to remember all the little things that will make your coffee house run smoother.

6.5.2 The Repair and Maintenance (R&M) Book

Your coffee house will have repair and maintenance issues. A coffee house has a lot of customer traffic going through it on a daily basis, as well as restaurant equipment that can get abused by your employees. When things break, they usually break on a Saturday or Sunday when it costs more to have it repaired. Or they may break during the busiest times. The best way to deal with problems as they come up is to have a good tool at your disposal, and I'm not talking about a wrench or a screwdriver. I'm talking about a Repair and Maintenance (R&M) book.

How to Create an R&M Book

Each piece of equipment in your coffee house will come with a manual. Keep these manuals in a safe place — preferably an equipment file so that you can refer to them for any replacement parts that you may need. The manuals will also be a great help in preparing your R&M book, as each piece of equipment will have its own maintenance needs.

The R&M book is not something that you check every day like the GM book but is rather a quick reference guide to use in emergencies. Consult this book before you call in a professional on emergencies such as a locked up cash register, a dripping faucet, or a warm refrigerator.

It takes time to build a good R&M book that is customized for your coffee house. To begin, look at all the things that could need repairing and find out ahead of time what you can do yourself to fix it.

Next, talk to some of your handy friends or, better yet, professionals, and ask them how to fix the problem.

In a notebook, create chapters relating to that piece of equipment. List the problem, probable cause, and how to fix it. For example, say the lights don't work in a part of the coffee house. Before you call an electrician, you go to your handy R&M book and look under:

Lighting

Problem:	None of the lights work in the dining room
Probable Cause:	Tripped circuit breaker
Repair:	Reset the breaker

Then you go to the breaker box and reset the breaker. It sounds simple, but if you asked an electrician how often they are called for a tripped breaker, you would be amazed.

Another simple one is a leaky faucet. Sooner or later, all faucets start to leak because of minerals in the water. Once the dripping starts, it wastes a lot of water and energy. To the customer, a dripping faucet says something subconsciously about the way you run your business. But before you call a plumber, go to your handy R&M book and look under:

Water

Problem:	Leaky faucet
Probable Cause:	Bad gasket
Repair:	Use Phillips head screwdriver and install new gasket

The job takes about five satisfying minutes to fix and costs you about 20 cents (the cost of the gasket).

Knowing that your cash register will most likely lock up at some point, you would talk to a technician to find out ways to reset the machine to get it to work again. If that fails, you would have a backup plan in your book that would involve a calculator and some hand-written checks.

When something breaks that you don't have the answer for, you will have to call in a professional to fix it. When that happens, you are presented with a golden opportunity to see how the problem was fixed and add that to your book. You might as well ask the professional a lot of other repair questions while they are at your place since you are paying for his time anyway.

As your business matures, so will your R&M book. It will be immensely helpful when the problems occur when you are not there and it is up to your assistants to decide whether to fix something or call in a professional. Over time, you can imagine how much money this proactive book can save you.

6.6 Bookkeeping System

Owning a coffee house means selling coffee, and that means taking in money. It is just as important to keep track of how that money comes in and goes out as it is to sell good coffee. A good bookkeeping system is at the heart of a good business.

The simplest way to do the books would be to take all your sales for the day, make up a deposit slip and take it to the bank. However, if you did this — and many businesses do — in the long run you would be making your life more difficult.

This is because you are selling much more than coffee. You are probably going to be selling food, perhaps beer or wine, and maybe some merchandise like hats, T-shirts, and coffee mugs. Don't forget that depending on where you live, you may be collecting a sales tax too. You have to keep track of all these types of sales separately.

Here is a simple system to do just that.

6.6.1 Create a Daily Sales Report

A Daily Sales Report (DSR) is simply your bookkeeping checklist. It lists all the possible categories of sales and incoming cash, and has a place to report your daily balance. A sample DSR form appears on the facing page. The CD-ROM that comes with this book includes a sample DSR form which you can print off to use in your business.

Sample Daily Sales Report Form

Daily Sales	Today	Month to Date
Coffee	$ _____	$ _____
Food	$ _____	$ _____
Other Beverages	$ _____	$ _____
Merchandise	$ _____	$ _____
Tax	$ _____	$ _____
Total	$ _____	$ _____
Cash	$ _____	$ _____
Checks	$ _____	$ _____
Credit Cards	$ _____	$ _____
Total	$ _____	$ _____
Over/Short	$ _____	$ _____
	Pace ___ / ___	$ _____

6.6.2 How to Use a DSR

Here is the step-by-step process you would follow to create and use your DSR:

- Start by ringing out your cash register. Depending on the type of cash register you have, the register will print up your totals according to what categories you have set up. Let's assume it prints totals for food, beverages, and merchandise. It will also give you a total for tax collected, if there is sales tax where you live.

- Transfer those totals to the top portion of your DSR.

- Count the money in your cash register drawer.

- Separate the cash from the checks and the credit card receipts. Start counting the cash (use a calculator that prints totals on paper tape), beginning with the largest denominations down to the pennies. Make an entry into the calculator for every level of denomination.

- When you have a total, subtract the money you leave in the register to start business with the next day. (If you start the day with an empty drawer, you will be unable to make change.) Let's assume you start with $150 made up of change and bills — nothing larger than a $5. Put this money back in the register.

- Put the leftover money into your deposit.

- Total the checks and enter that amount into the DSR.

- When you close out your credit card machine (your credit card company will show you how this works) it will print up a total of the credit cards for the day. Record that amount on your DSR and save the credit card receipts in a separate place for future reference.

- Finally, add all the types of revenue you collected to come up with a total. That total should match your total sales for the day.

6.6.3 Correcting Errors

What if the actual money you count doesn't match your cash register receipt? Mistakes can happen in many places:

- Your change bank (this is a separate box of money you use to make change out of — a good amount would be $300 or $400)

- Your cash drawer (we said it was $150)

- Your deposit (your sales for the day)

If you are short in your deposit, you must be over in one of the other two areas.

For example, if you finish your deposit and discover that your change bank is $20 short, most likely you are $20 over in your deposit or your cash drawer. The remedy would be to re-count those to locate the missing $20.

The exception to this would be a mistake at the cash register; for instance, if someone gave the wrong change or didn't adjust for an item that was mistakenly rung up. It is a lot tougher to find these mistakes. However, if you look first to the money triangle, you will find the majority of your mistakes.

How to Make Fewer Errors

To assure that there are fewer mistakes when you do your books, always use the same process every day. I start by counting my change bank and finish by signing and dating the calculator tape I added my totals on. It's sort of like my guarantee that everything has checked out. I place the tape in the change bank with the money. The next time the money is counted, whoever does the counting knows when it was counted last and that it was counted correctly.

Recording Your Pace

At the very bottom of your DSR, there is a place to record your pace. Your pace is an estimate of what you hope to do in sales in any given time – for our example, one month – based on the sales your have done so far in the month. It is based on a fraction, as in 5/31, or, in other words 5 days out of 31.

As an easy example, let's say that at the end of Day 5 you have done $5,000. Using this formula, you would take the total sales month to date ($5,000), and divide it by how many days so for that month ($5,000 ÷ 5). This gives you average daily sales of $1,000. Now take that average daily sales figure and multiply it by the total number of days in the month ($1,000 x 31) and this will give you a total of $31,000.

Assuming you continue to average $1,000 per day, you will have a pretty good idea of how much sales you will do for the month. You will know on a daily basis how well you're doing, instead of waiting until the end of the month. Armed with this information, you can now make adjustments in labor or start new promotions to boost sales. As we will get into in chapter 7, this works into the budget process so that you can plan your profits instead of just hoping for the best.

When you are done with your books, take the printout from the cash register that you used to record your sales information, and staple it to the back of your DSR. This will give you a way to verify that the sales you recorded on your DSR are the same as the sales recorded on your cash register. This will come in to play when you do your audits, which will be explained in section 7.5.

6.7 The Manager Meeting

This guide outlines a variety of systems that will keep your coffee house consistent and looking good. For example, chapter 7 explains how to budget and earlier sections in this chapter describe systems for soliciting customer feedback so you can improve and keep changing with the times. What you need now is a way to synthesize all these systems into a way to change. This can be easily accomplished through a manager meeting.

In a manager meeting, you bring all of the previous systems together and make changes! The secret to letting your coffee house grow and be competitive is to keep it changing while preserving the basic infrastructure.

A manager meeting is a good way to stop your busy schedule once a week to take stock and focus on the business as a whole. It is a time to step back a little bit and look at the big picture. This is an important step to getting away from the day-to-day minutia of running a business.

However, most meetings are a waste of time. This is because most of the time spent in meetings is spent gossiping about employees, customers, sports, or whatever. The key in a meeting is to set a time limit and write down an agenda. If you finish early, there will be plenty of time for gossip.

6.7.1 Tips for Running a Meeting

There are good and bad ways to run a meeting. Here are five suggestions to help keep your meetings running smoothly:

- Try not to schedule the meetings early in the mornings when one of the participants closed late the previous night.

- Try to schedule the meeting during a slow time of the day, in the middle of the week or at the slowest time of the week. Look at your sales to figure out when it is slowest. Your cash register probably can print up a report on sales by the hour. You want to avoid being interrupted because the business is slammed. You need to concentrate and stick to the agenda.

- If possible, don't schedule a meeting on someone's day off. There should be at least one day that everyone is there.

- Pick a place that is far enough away from your customers that they can't hear you or see you talking about them and your profits. Your customers shouldn't know all the dirty details about running the coffee house.

- Pick a consistent time every week. That way, the meetings will become a habit for you and your employees, and people will be less likely to disturb you during the meeting.

So what do you go over at the meeting? Everything! You need to go over all the important parts of your operating system (see section 7.5.1). Think of this meeting as your business tune-up.

If an external audit was completed (see section 7.5.3), spend a lot more time going over this. See how you can make changes to the current checklists to accommodate any problems that show up.

6.7.2 Items to Cover in the Manager Meeting

Assignments

Go over any assignments that you gave out at the last meeting. Perhaps a new checklist has to be made, a new promotion handled, or research must be done to find ways to save on utilities. If you give out assignments without following up, it just won't work. Hold people accountable. Always make this the first thing to go over at your meeting.

Audits

Have the managers turn in their audits for the past week. Spend a few minutes going over each problem and make an immediate change to do something about it. If the external audit consistently shows that the windows are dirty, analyze how you are cleaning them. If it is twice a week, change it to everyday.

The Scoreboard

A scoreboard is a way of keeping track of profits in the day-to-day operation of your coffee house (this will be covered in more detail in section 7.4.4).

At the manager's meeting, you'll want to review your scoreboard. Talk about the numbers and whether or not you are hitting your targets. What kinds of ideas can you come up with to improve them if you are not meeting your targets? This gets everyone involved in the game. The work you do now will ensure a problem doesn't grow out of hand by the end of the month.

If you go over the budget numbers, you may see that your sales are going to be short by $1,000. If you have three weeks left in the month, that equals an extra $47.61 per day you need to make up. If you are open for twelve hours, that is roughly $4 extra per hour. Putting something on special and featuring it at the cash register might accomplish this. You only need to sell one per hour. Because of the manager meeting, you have recognized this.

Customer Comment Cards and E-mails

Read the customer comment cards and any e-mails you have received — whether they were good or bad. It is a morale booster to read the good ones. For the bad ones, discuss possible solutions to the problems pointed out by the customer. Relay the ideas you come up with back to the customer. They will appreciate it!

Your meeting shouldn't last more than an hour. Whatever time you set aside for your meeting should be treated with the respect it deserves. Don't waste that time.

It is very important for a business to change with the times and respond as fast as possible to trends, market conditions, and how the business is perceived in the community. By meeting once a week to go over all the details of the operation system, you have the means to make changes immediately so the following week will be better.

7. Budgets and Building Wealth

7.1 Why a Budget is Essential

For most of us, being in business is about being our own boss, having fun, and making a profit. Granted, some people might go into business just for something to do, but if they were not concerned about making a profit, they would not remain in business long. Financially speaking, profit helps define the difference between success and failure.

Profit is not a dirty word. If you don't make a profit, you cannot pay yourself or your employees, let alone give raises and benefits. You will have a hard time keeping up with the maintenance of your coffee house and it will start to fall apart. You didn't get into business to fail. If you really want to succeed, you need all the tools you can get in order to achieve your goal.

Budgets are one of the most effective tools to help you succeed. Can you name one successful company that does not have a budget? With a budget, you have more control of the cash going out of your business. Remember the old saying, "It's not how much you make but how much you keep."

When we started our first restaurant, we would go through our month making deposits, doing our inventories, and taking care of our customers. At the end of the month, we would put all of our monthly financial information together and send it off to our accountant. He would get the information by the seventh of the month, then do his part and get it back to us in the form of a Profit and Loss (P&L) statement by the fifteenth.

The problem with this system is that the information was already so old, it didn't do a whole lot of good. If it showed that we didn't make any money, that month was already history. In fact, the current month was already half over. What we needed was information in real time. We needed a P&L at the beginning of the month. We call this P&L a budget!

7.1.1 Profit and Loss (P&L) Statement

Create your own P&L at the beginning of the month. This will tell you what your sales are, the cost of sales, and all your expenses (to the best of your knowledge). Then you try to make this a reality.

Believe me, it's much more likely to happen if you start down this road at the beginning of the month with a road map. Your budget, your P&L, is your road map. Here's how you do it.

Prioritize

A P&L is laid out for you like a priority list. The items on the list include the following:

Sales

Without sales, you cannot stay in business. Money coming in is fuel for the machine. By working on promoting your business, providing value to your customers, and so on, you develop your sales potential.

Cost of Sales

How much do you spend on the raw product – coffee, bulk food, and other items – you are selling? This involves controls by keeping track of inventories, theft prevention, smart purchasing, and many other factors.

Labor

With the exception of the raw products you are selling, labor will be your biggest expense.

80/20 Principle

An Italian mathematician, Vilfredo Pareto (1848-1923), came up with what is now referred to as the 80/20 principle. Basically, the 80/20 principle states that 80 percent of your results come from 20 percent of your effort. Translated into a P&L, it means that by concentrating on sales, cost of sales, and labor, you will produce the majority of your profit.

For example, if you had just one hour a week extra to spend on your coffee house, would it be better spent on coming up with a new sales promotion or researching a different style of trash bag to purchase that is less expensive? In other words, the one hour spent on sales could bring in an extra $1,000 for the month, while the trash bag savings – while important – would only save you $25!

Or how about looking into a new menu item that would yield a better food cost or a new way to schedule that could save a couple of labor hours a day? By prioritizing your precious time and applying the 80/20 principle, you will go further at a faster speed. We are always concentrating our effort on what will bring our business the greatest good for the least amount of effort. Once we understand this, it will make building a budget more meaningful. Let's look a little closer at our P&L to better understand the impact of this priority list.

7.1.2 Managing Sales

Sales are the foundation of any business. Remember, "No sales, no business." So how do we manage sales? One way is to quantify it.

The longer you are in business, the more numbers and data you will collect. This includes keeping track of your sales figures. After you have a full year under your belt, it will become easier to predict your sales for the current year. This will help you to know if your sales are growing or shrinking.

Comparing your current sales to that of the prior month isn't really accurate, because sales fluctuate throughout the year based on seasonal trends like summer break, Christmas, and tax time. You can't really estimate what January is going to be like until you have experienced a January. It certainly isn't going to be like December, when the hordes are out shopping.

To find out what your sales are going to be, interview other business owners and find out what their busy times of the year are. Once you have a month or two of sales, you can best judge if the next month will be busier or slower, depending on what you have learned from other businesses. All this becomes so much easier once you have a whole year's worth of sales to look back on. After you have reached this milestone, creating your budget will be a breeze.

Sales will be the first item on your budget. You'll want to look at the prior year's sales for the month, and then look at the trends of the current year. Are your sales from last year up an average of 5 percent? If so, add 5 percent to what you predict you will do in sales for the current month. You can then make any other adjustments, such as for construction on the street in front of your coffee house, or a large convention in town that brings in lots of extra business.

Other factors to look at are things like the calendar. The number of weekends in the month will affect your business. Special holidays or long weekends can add or subtract from your sales as well.

7.1.3 Cost of Sales and Inventory

First, you need to know what the things you sell are costing you. The best way to do this is with an inventory. Inventories are a necessary evil. Many business owners get into trouble because they do not keep track of their inventories. How can you hope to stay in business if you don't have a firm grip on what you are selling? It's all about inventory control and, other than sales, it is the most important thing you can do for your business.

To calculate cost of sales you use the following formula:

Beginning Inventory + Purchases – Ending Inventory = Cost of Sales

Take the number you end up with and divide it by your sales to come up with a cost of sales as a percent. This is a very important figure in your budget.

Let's discuss each component of the formula above.

The first thing you need to do is to establish a beginning inventory. Do this on the first day of the month. Take inventory of all the things you sell – such as bulk coffee, syrups, milk, etc. – and then multiply each item by what the item costs per unit (your cost). Next, add all the total columns to come up with a total value of the inventory. This will give you your current inventory in dollars.

Say you do a beginning inventory, and you determined that you had 25 pounds of coffee in stock. At a purchase price of $5.90, this means you have $147.50 worth of coffee on hand.

As the month continues, let's say you purchase another 50 pounds of coffee. At $5.90 per pound, that's $295.00. At the end of the month, you take an ending inventory and you have 15 pounds left. That's $88.50 worth of coffee.

Using the formula, here's how you would figure out your cost of sales:

$147.50 *(beginning inventory)* + $295.00 *(purchases)* – $88.50 *(ending inventory)* = $354.00 *(cost of sales)*

Now let's say you sell the coffee for $1.25 a cup, and during the month, you sold 2,360 cups. This would give you $2,950.00 in total sales.

To calculate your cost of sales as a percentage, simply divide your cost of sales by your total sales.

$354.00 *(cost of sales)* ÷ $2,950.00 *(total sales)* = .12

The figures above would give you a 12 percent cost of sales.

This example has outlined how to determine your cost of sales using only one item — coffee. On your actual inventory sheet, you will need to determine the sales figures for all of the different items you sell. You can combine all the items together and come up with one total cost, or you can break the figures into categories, such as food, beverages, and merchandise.

You would then have a separate inventory sheet for every one of these categories, with the total from all the categories as your overall cost. By breaking your inventory down into categories, it will be easier to examine problems in specific areas if you fail to meet your target percentages.

Here is an example of a food inventory sheet. On your own inventory sheet, you will need to update the prices of the inventory as they change. Amounts for items like produce change almost weekly. Prices for spices stay pretty consistent. Your inventory should have the most up-to-date prices as they reflect the current value of your inventory.

Sample Food Inventory Sheet

Part 1: Food

Dry Goods

Item	Count	Amount	Price	Total
Almond Extract	oz.	2	$ 2.00	$ 4.00
Almonds	lb.	2.5	38.10	95.25
Artichoke Hearts	can	1	10.00	10.00
Baking Cocoa	lb.	3	5.34	16.02
Baking Powder	can	0.5	8.30	4.15
Basil	oz.	1.5	.80	1.20
Basmati Rice	lb.	18	.35	6.30
Black Beans	can	2	5.32	10.64
Black Olives	can	1.25	8.35	10.44
Bow Tie Pasta	box	32	1.90	60.80
Brown Sugar	lb.	13	.43	5.59
Cardomon	oz.	1	.45	.45
Cayenne Pepper	oz.	3	.45	1.35
Chicken Broth	can	18	3.00	54.00
Chocolate	lb.	10	1.90	19.00
Chocolate Chips	lb.	6	2.24	13.44
Cilantro	oz.	1.25	.62	.78
Cinnamon Sticks	oz.	1.5	.40	.60
Cloves	oz.	2.1	.65	1.37
Corn Meal	lb.	13	.30	3.90
Cumin	oz.	1	.40	.40
Curry	oz.	1.4	.40	.56
Dill	oz.	1.2	.62	.74
Evaporated Milk	can	5	.95	4.75

Flour, Wheat	lb.	75	$ .19	$ 14.25
Flour, White	lb.	150	.12	18.00
Garbonzo Beans	can	3	3.92	11.76
Garlic	oz.	1.25	.58	.73
Ginger	oz.	1.25	.54	.68
Ketchup	ea.	18	.82	14.76
Mustard	ea.	20	.65	13.00
Oil, Olive	gal.	4	7.96	31.84
Oil, Vegetable	gal.	5	3.27	16.35
Pecans	lb.	6	4.78	28.68
Pepper, Black	oz.	8	.50	4.00
Pepper, White	oz.	4	.76	3.04
Pine Nuts	lb.	12	3.75	45.00
Poppy Seeds	oz.	4	.31	1.24
Raisins	lb.	12	1.80	21.60
Salt	lb.	25	.06	1.50
Semolina	lb.	50	.23	11.50
Sugar	lb.	45	.19	8.55
Sun-dried Tomatoes	lb.	1	6.00	6.00
Sweet & Low	lb.	1.5	.32	.48
Tarragon	oz.	1	1.95	1.95
Thyme	oz.	1	.50	.50
Tobasco	ea.	12	.68	8.16
Tomato, Crushed	can	6	4.66	27.96
Tomato, Diced	can	6	3.95	23.70
Tuna	can	8	2.15	17.20
Vinegar	ea.	2	3.00	6.00
Walnuts	lb.	2.25	5.45	12.26
Yeast	lb.	2.4	3.25	7.80

Total Dry Goods   **$ 684.22**

Produce

Item	Count	Amount	Price	Total
Basil	*lb.*	1	$ 3.25	$ 3.25
Broccoli	*lb.*	6	.72	4.32
Carrots	*lb.*	12	.45	5.40
Garlic	*lb.*	5	5.50	27.50
Mushrooms	*lb.*	8	3.18	25.44
Onions, Red	*lb.*	40	.07	2.80
Onions, Yellow	*lb.*	35	.08	2.80
Oregano	*lb.*	1.2	3.75	4.50
Red Bells	*ea.*	3	.62	1.86
Red Leaf	*ea.*	24	.92	22.08
Romaine	*ea.*	20	.92	18.40
Tomatoes	*ea.*	30	.45	13.50

Total Produce   **$ 131.85**

Meat and Dairy

Item	Count	Amount	Price	Total
Asiago	*lb.*	6	$ 2.08	$ 12.48
Blue	*lb.*	4	2.85	11.40
Butter	*lb.*	18	2.13	38.34
Butter Packets	*lb.*	12.25	2.36	28.91
Cheddar	*lb.*	7.5	1.90	14.25
Chicken	*lb.*	20	1.90	38.00
Eggs	*ea.*	54	.06	3.24
Feta	*lb.*	3.5	3.20	11.20
Ham	*lb.*	10	2.25	22.50
Mayonnaise	*gal.*	2.5	10.49	26.23

Item	Count	Amount	Price	Total
Milk	gal.	5	$ 3.25	$ 16.25
Mozzarella	lb.	26	1.48	38.48
Roast Beef	lb.	15	1.80	27.00
Skim Milk	gal.	3.25	3.25	10.56
Turkey	lb.	6	24.00	144.00

Total Meat and Dairy   **$ 442.84**

Part 2: Beverages

Item	Count	Amount	Price	Total
Blue Sky Sodas	ea.	36	$ .37	$ 13.32
Chai	gal.	2.25	16.37	36.83
Chai Decaf	gal.	1.5	16.37	24.56
Columbian	lb.	11	5.10	56.10
Costa Rican Terazu	lb.	7	6.00	42.00
Decaf	lb.	24	5.20	124.80
Espresso Blend	lb.	18	5.10	91.80
Espresso Decaf	lb.	6.25	5.20	32.50
Ethiopean Harrar	lb.	10	6.00	60.00
Fresh Orange Juice	gal.	3.5	4.25	14.88
Guatamalan Atitlan	lb.	5	5.90	29.50
House Blend	lb.	25	5.10	127.50
Kenyan AA	lb.	5	6.20	31.00
Kona	lb.	6	13.00	78.00
Mexican Gustapec	lb.	12	5.10	61.20
Nicaraguan Jimotega	lb.	5	5.75	28.75

Total Beverages   **$ 852.74**

Part 3: Merchandise

Item	Count	Amount	Price	Total
Coffee Mugs	ea.	49	$ .75	$ 36.75
Hats	ea.	30	6.00	180.00
Long Sleeve	ea.	48	7.50	360.00
Short Sleeve	ea.	60	6.50	390.00
Sweat Shirt	ea.	24	9.95	238.80
To-Go Mugs	ea.	36	1.25	45.00

Total Merchandise   **$ 1,250.55**

Totals

	Food	Beverages	Merch.
Beginning Inventory	$ 1,356.20	$ 782.00	$ 1,600.50
Purchases	1,438.41	682.47	0.00
Ending Inventory	1,258.91	852.74	1,250.55
Cost of Goods Sold	1,535.70	611.73	349.95
Sales	5,589.70	5,780.20	770.00
Percentages	**27.48**	**10.58**	**45.45**

7.2 Labor Costs

It is almost impossible to avoid labor costs. Even if it is just you in your business, you must pay yourself something! Outside of the products you actually buy to sell, labor is your biggest expense. Every dollar you save here goes right to the bottom line and then some.

There are two ways to figure out your labor costs: by percentage or by actual cost.

7.2.1 Labor Cost by Percentage

To find your labor costs by percentage, divide the cost of labor for any given period (say, a month) by sales in that same period.

Let's say you spent $7,700 last month on wages. Your sales were $35,000 (taxes not included; they are not sales). Divide $7,700 by $35,000, which equals 22 percent. This means for every dollar you took in, you spent 22 cents in labor.

If you establish that your monthly labor cost is 22 percent, then you would multiply whatever number you hope to be your monthly sales in your budget by 22 percent. That will give you the total you can spend on labor.

7.2.2 Labor Formula by Actual Cost

Another way you can figure out your labor budget is to schedule based on the actual cost of the labor. You will know the minimum number of people needed to operate your coffee house, so just multiply their hours by what they make an hour.

There will be a minimum number of labor hours needed, but there should also be a maximum as well. This will be reflected in varying labor percentages. If sales are low, then your labor cost will be high as a percentage. If your sales go through the roof, then it will reflect in a very low labor cost.

7.2.3 Labor Saving Tips

Taking a schedule-based approach to budgeting your labor costs is a good starting point. If, after you have created your budget, it looks like you are going to be in the red, then you can go back and change the schedule to try to cut hours by being more creative where you can.

By using the percentage method, it might be fine to hope for a 22 percent labor cost, but if you only predict $20,000 in sales instead of $35,000, you've lost $3,300 you can spend in labor. That's not too easy to work with, even though you may have to.

Here are some ideas you can start off with to save you money on labor:

- Try alternating arrival and departure times for employees. Concentrate your labor for when you have the most sales. Stagger the times your employees come to work and when they leave. This puts the most employees on duty when it is the busiest.

- Pay your best people a little more, but have them cover during slow times so that you can eliminate a person entirely. You could have one morning person and one night person with a good employee who comes in a little later in the morning and works into the night shift through the busy times, instead of two morning people and two night people. It gives you the same coverage while eliminating one position.

- Assign extra responsibilities to management — small things that can be done in place of an extra person coming in to do them.

- By using your checklist system, you can assign extra work to your core employees to cover for some duties of other employees, allowing them to come in later or not at all.

Managing labor is one of the most crucial things you can do for your business. It is also one of the most difficult, mainly because personalities are involved and you are dealing with people's livelihood. This is why you budget in the first place—to keep the business as healthy as possible and ensure that everyone can have a livelihood.

7.3 Other Expenses

We have covered the most important aspects of a profitable P&L, but there is a long way to go before you reach the net profit figure. Here are some expenses that are typical in a coffee house P&L statement.

I've divided them into two areas: controllable and noncontrollable. It may seem obvious, but controllable expenses are those you can control, while noncontrollable expenses are those you can't control.

7.3.1 Controllable Expenses

Labor Taxes

Labor taxes are controllable because every dollar you save on labor is a dollar you don't have to pay labor taxes on. Payroll taxes can cost anywhere from 12 percent to 18 percent of your total payroll.

Repair and Maintenance

We covered this in section 6.5.2 on R&M Books. The more you are on top of this, the better. You should look at this as Repair and Preventative Maintenance. In your budget, though, you should allow some money for the repairs that will come up.

Supplies

These are all the items you need to run your coffee house. From time to time, look at all of them and try to find less expensive alternatives. If you find a better and cheaper trash bag that costs five cents less a piece, and you go through a hundred bags a month, that's a savings of $60 a year. Sixty dollars would make a nice Christmas bonus for a dishwasher, and for no extra work.

Other areas to save on are register paper, ink ribbons, and other office supplies. Be careful when you're in an office supply store; you'll see all sorts of things you think you can't live without.

Advertising

Advertising costs will fluctuate depending on what time of year it is or what you want to push. Some advertising expenses come up every month, such as the Yellow Pages or the fees for your website. Big companies allocate as much as five percent of gross receipts towards advertising. You may spend hardly anything and instead use creativity to reach potential customers.

Equipment Rental

This is for anything you can rent, like ice machines or dishwashers.

Replacement

This category is different from supplies because it is used for actually replacing items that are not just for one-time use. This would include things like glassware, silverware, and china. If you notice that your replacement expenses are continually rising, you may want to look at a different type of drinking glass that doesn't break as often. Or you may want to create a better system so that the dishwashers don't accidentally throw out silverware with the food scraps.

Utilities

Utilities can add up in no time. Many owners and managers walk into their business at 8:00 a.m. and immediately flick on every light in the place, even if they won't be open to the public until 10:00 a.m. Multiply those extra hours by each light bulb in your coffee house, and think about how much electricity you're paying for by turning on the lights early.

You will no doubt get some products that come in frozen. The health department requires you to defrost by running the product under a constant stream of water. Think about how much water that wastes! The other alternative is to use your checklists so that the day before the item needs to be used, it is taken from the freezer and placed in the refrigerator. This will save you a lot of money in water costs, as well as a lot of time that you would otherwise spend defrosting products underwater.

Music

Whether you pay for live entertainment or use recorded music, this is something you'll want for your coffee house.

There are music services like satellite, cable, Muzak, or other similar services. If you choose to just buy CDs and play them, you are required to pay an ASCAP fee for the royalties. The fee will vary depending on how you plan to use the music. Visit **www.ascap.com** for more information.

The only way around the ASCAP fees is if you get the personal permission from the artists. While it may not be that easy to get Eric

Clapton to give you permission to play his music, you could do what Bill Mehaffey does at Bongo Billy's. He uses local artists and those of the PutaMayo world music label (**www.putamayo.com**), and then sells their CDs at his coffee houses. You could also find local talent and sell their CDs.

Telephone

Telephone expenses can be greater than you think. Use phones that can restrict all long distance calls at the bar, while still allowing you to make them from the office. Have your phone company tell you how to set this up.

7.3.2 Noncontrollable Expenses

Every business has expenses that really cannot be controlled. They have to be figured in if you are going to produce a preview P&L statement. Only until you have all the numbers plugged in can you see if there will be anything left over that could be considered profit. For example:

- Business loans — Only interest is reported on an actual P&L, but for budget purposes it is best to use the whole figure. On your P&L, you are not allowed to expense out the principal on a loan because it was never your money to begin with. You are just paying it back, so your only true expense is the interest you are paying. For your needs, you are still writing that check and it is money coming out of your cash flow. We need to account for it here.

- Depreciation — Depreciation is something you can expense out, according to the IRS, but it is not actually money you are spending in the month. You spent it already in one large chunk and are spreading that expense over a longer period. Leave this figure out. We are only concerned with money that is actually being spent.

- Credit card fees — Even though you can negotiate for lower fees, you can't really control credit card fees unless you make your customers pay in cash.

- Other items — Rent, insurance, legal fees, accounting fees, etc.

With this information, you can create a P&L for the next month by plugging in all the numbers you know for a fact or can assume using historical information. If it shows a profit and you think it is fair, leave it alone. If it doesn't, or you think the profit isn't good enough, you can go back and adjust some of the numbers to bring the whole P&L into line with your expectations. This is your working budget. Now you have to make it happen.

When you are done, it will look something like this:

Sample Profit and Loss Statement

Sales

Total Sales	$ 40,000.00
Cost of Sales @ 25%	- $ 10,000.00

Gross Profit	*$ 30,000.00*

Labor

Labor @ 28%	$ 11,200.00

Total Labor	*$ 11,200.00*

Noncontrollable Expenses

Labor Taxes	$ 1,344.00
Supplies	+ $ 1,500.00
Replacement	+ $ 250.00
Advertising	+ $ 1,500.00
Equipment Rental	+ $ 300.00
Repair and Maintenance	+ $ 500.00
Music	+ $ 35.00
Telephone	+ $ 225.00
Utilities	+ $ 1,200.00

Total Noncontrollable Expenses	*$ 6,854.00*

continued on next page

Controllable Expenses

Credit Card Fees	$ 600.00
Insurance	+ $ 800.00
Legal	+ $ 0.00
Accounting	+ $ 350.00
Rent	+ $ 1,500.00
Bank Loan	+ $ 4,000.00

Total Controllable Expenses	$ 7,250.00

Net Profit

Gross Profit	$ 30,000.00
Total Labor @ 28%	- $ 11,200.00
Total Noncontrollable Expenses	- $ 6,854.00
Total Controllable Expenses	- $ 7,250.00

Total Net Profit	$ 4,696.00

7.4 Tracking Sales

In this section, we will examine how to arrive at some of the figures we need in order to track sales. We will also see how to put these figures on a score board so that everyone on your staff can know how business is doing.

7.4.1 Sales Pace

The sales pace is the pace the business is on if it continues to run at its current average sales volume. The formula works like this:

(Total Sales ÷ Number of Business Days So Far in Month) x Total Number of Business Days in Month = Sales Pace

Let's say on day 18 of the month that you have done $42,387.22 in sales. (Your daily sales report, covered in section 6.6.1, will show you this figure.) Divide this number by 17 (the seventeen full days of prior sales), which will equal $2,493.36. This is your daily average. Next, multiply this number by the total number of business days in the month, which in this case is 31, and your projected sales for the month is $77,294.16.

Say you had budgeted $75,000 for sales at the beginning of the month, based on sales of $72,750 for the same month last year and a three percent growth rate. Now you have two figures:

- Your budget of $75,000

- Your current sales pace of $77,294.16

Pretty good so far.

7.4.2 Cost of Sales

This is one thing you probably can't check every day. If you remember from section 7.1.3, you have to do inventory in order to figure out your cost of sales.

To review, you use the following formula to obtain the cost of sales:

Beginning Inventory + Purchases – Ending Inventory = Cost of Sales

Divide this figure by the corresponding sales for the inventory period, which will yield your cost as a percentage. This percentage is an important figure that you will write down on your scoreboard along with the date of the last time you calculated it.

7.4.3 Labor

We discussed how to determine your monthly labor costs in section 7.2. To review, you can do this in two ways:

- By percentage — Divide the cost of labor for a month by the sales in that same period.

- By actual cost — Add up the hours worked by everyone in your coffee house, then multiply by their wages per hour.

Calculating Daily Labor Budget

After you have figured out what your monthly labor budget is, divide that figure by the number of days you are going to be open during the month. This will give you your daily labor budget. You can compare this figure against what you actually spent.

To calculate your daily labor, just write down the number of hours your employees work every day and multiply it by their wage. You can make up a worksheet to do this, or buy a cash register that can clock your employees in and out and generate a daily report.

If you have employees that are on salary, like you, take that total and divide it by the number of days per month. This daily total is then added to your other total wages for a grand total.

Labor Bank

Your labor bank is like a virtual bank account that helps you keep track of your labor budget. It's a running total of how much you're actually spending on labor, and it's a great tool that allows you to make adjustments on the fly and stay within your budget.

Let's say your budget allows you to spend $500 a day on labor. If your total labor cost for the first day of the month was $499, then you have $1 left over. This dollar is "deposited" in your labor bank.

The next day, you spend $550 on labor, which is $50 more than you had budgeted. You need to "withdraw" this money from your labor bank. Since you had a balance of $1 the day before, your balance is now negative $49.

You know you are $49 over your labor budget. To make up for it, the next day you let some employees off 15 minutes early. Because of that, you only spend $460 that day — $40 under what you originally budgeted.

Combine this $40 with the negative $49 in your labor bank, and now you're only $9 over your labor budget for the month. You know how much you need to save tomorrow in order to get back on track.

As you go through the month, you will find that it is easy to save when the numbers are right in front of you. This is real money. If you come to the end of the month and you have a positive balance, you will have some cash for bonuses for those who worked extra hard during the month.

7.4.4 Your Scoreboard

Can you imagine playing baseball and not keeping score? What would be the fun in that?

Well, that is usually how people go about their businesses: playing each inning every day without knowing if they are winning or losing the game.

To make things more interesting in our day-to-day operation of your coffee house, you will want to create a scoreboard that will tell you the score – your profit – on a daily basis.

For our example, we'll rely on the 80/20 principal and just concentrate on the big three: sales, cost of sales, and labor. If the scoreboard shows that you are hitting your targets in these areas, then you should be 80 percent of the way toward profitability.

How to Create Your Own Scoreboard

Buy a large dry-erase board and put it up in your office where you will see it every day.

At the top of the board, write today's date. Down the side of the board, write your sales budget figure and sales pace. Also write the cost of sales percentages that you calculated from your most recent inventory. At the bottom of the board, make a section for your labor bank.

Sample Scoreboard

As of: (day) / (month) / (year)

Sales Budget: $ 70,000.00

Sales Pace: $ 71,482.32

Cost of Sales:
   Food: 27.48%
   Beverages: 10.58%
   Merchandise: 45.45%

Labor Bank: − $ 23.00

Using Your Scoreboard

It's Monday morning. You walk into your coffee house after taking Saturday and Sunday off and leaving your managers in charge for the weekend. The first thing you do is check your scoreboard.

You see your sales budget of $70,000 and a sales pace of $71,482.32. The cost of sales is up to date and running within your target margins. The labor bank shows negative $23.00 — apparently the managers aren't as good as you when it comes to getting people off the clock. But other than that, the numbers look great! You can take up the labor problem at the next manager's meeting.

There you have it. You know what the score is. You know if your coffee house is winning or losing without having to wait for the end of the month and into the next one for the accountant to produce a P&L. You have your finger on the pulse of your business in real time. You are running it well, thanks to your checklists. You are hiring better, too.

Things look rosy, but how do you keep it this way day in and day out? Will everyone continue to do their checklists? Will employees really be trained according to your systems? Will the managers keep up with the scoreboard on a daily basis like you would? In order to know for sure, you will need to audit.

7.5 Audits

One of the hardest things to do personally and in business is to be consistent. We promise ourselves all sorts of things, from new exercise programs, to reading one book per week, to vowing to eat healthier. And we do it for a couple of weeks, until something interrupts our new routine and the whole thing falls by the wayside.

What we need is someone who will hold us accountable. This is especially true if you are your own boss, and you want all your hard work to pay off. I have found that the best way to make sure everything is getting done is with an audit system.

7.5.1 The Internal Audit

An internal audit is basically a checklist of things that should be done on an ongoing basis. With this audit, you will see if all your systems are working and that your managers and staff are doing their jobs.

Determine How the Coffee House Should Look

First, assign an area of your coffee house to a manager (or yourself, if you are the only one managing). Make a list of how the area should look. Include everything you can think of — the cleanliness of the light fixtures, the walls and floors, the artwork that should hang straight, and other things.

Financial Information

You should also include financial information that reflects your scoreboard. Every manager has a hand in this. If the cost of sales is high, it is important to find out the cause and make adjustments as soon as possible. If your sales are just under what was predicted in your budget, then it is every manager's responsibility to do whatever they can to increase sales. The financial items on the audit sheets are the same for every manager.

Weekly Audits

Do audits once a week and turn them in at the weekly manager's meeting. It doesn't matter when during the week the audit is performed, nor does it matter what time of day. It just needs to happen at some point, and will probably take only 15 to 30 minutes to do.

Everyone who does an audit needs to be honest in what they see. If something is not getting done in their area as often as needed, they can change an employee's checklist to make sure the job gets done well enough to reflect in the next audit.

But to make it more fun (and to be able to relate the audit to bonuses), it needs to be scored.

7.5.2 Scoring The Audit

Wouldn't it be an improvement if work could turn into a game? Stocking widgets on a shelf is work. Stocking widgets on a shelf but doing it faster than the guy next to you is fun! Work can become a game, if you know the rules.

There is an excellent book I recommend called *The Game Of Work*, by Charles A. Coonradt. The author wonders why people would complain about how physically hard their work is and then go play football on the weekend and get totally beat up! The answer is simple: One is a game and the other isn't. Turning work into a game is the idea behind scoring audits.

There are a few guidelines you must follow to create a good game:

- Keep score

- Post the scores

- Put the players in charge of the scores

- Make sure everyone knows the rules, and don't change them

- List the rewards and penalties, and stick to them

How to Score the Audit

An easy way to keep score is to assign values to each item on the audit sheet. For example, dusting the lights could be worth two points while meeting the sales budget could be worth 15. I like to use a system where all the values add up to 100, because it's easy to understand and gives you quite a bit of flexibility. What each item is worth depends on what you think is important. However, it is best to emphasize the most important three items — sales, cost of sales, and labor.

Once you have assigned numbers to your categories, you need to think of a scoring system. Here is one suggestion, based on a system where everything adds up to 100:

Number of Points	Grade
100–90	100%
89–80	90%
79–70	80%
69–Below	Fail

It will be difficult to get 100 points on an audit, but if the score is 90 or above, the system is working. If you score below 70 points, someone isn't doing their job. If you score anywhere in between, you're not doing bad, but the system needs improving. If you are doing audits once a week, you can take the average of the scores for the month and use that to help calculate bonuses.

You can take a look at a sample audit sheet on the next page. But no matter how much you trust your people to do their audits accurately, you need a system to check up on them. This is where an external audit comes in.

7.5.3 The External Audit

Even the best plans have holes in them. There will be times when you or the managers just don't feel like following the systems or doing your internal audit sincerely. It might be that there just isn't enough time, or that something else more important comes up. These are the times that can cause the whole system to break down.

One of the best ways to insure that the audits are done accurately is to instigate an external audit. This audit will be done to verify that the other audits are correct and therefore that the system is working.

Sample Audit Sheet (With Scoring)

Dining Room	Points Possible	Points Awarded
Floors Clean	2	_____
Baseboards Clean	2	_____
Walls Clean	2	_____
Table Bases Clean	2	_____
Chairs Clean	2	_____
Lights Dusted	2	_____
All Light Bulbs Working	2	_____
Ceiling Clean	2	_____
Vents Clean	2	_____
Pictures Hung Straight	2	_____
Windows Clean	2	_____

Restrooms	Points Possible	Points Awarded
Floors Clean	2	_____
Baseboards Clean	2	_____
Walls Clean	2	_____
Ceiling Clean	2	_____
Toilets Clean	2	_____
Sink Clean	2	_____
Sink Fixture Clean	2	_____
Lights Dusted	2	_____
All Light Bulbs Working	2	_____
Vents Clean	2	_____
Door Clean	2	_____

Financial	Points Possible	Points Awarded
Scoreboard Up To Date	10	_____
Food Cost 22%	10	_____
Coffee Cost 15%	10	_____
Beverage Cost 28%	10	_____
Merchandise Cost 55%	4	_____
Employee Files Up To Date	4	_____
Office Clean	4	_____
All Paperwork Filed	4	_____

Total Score _____

Date: _____

Manager: _____

The external audit is like the internal audits, but it is performed by someone from the outside. The object of an external audit, after all, is to keep you and your managers in check. Train a friend or family member to do it so that your personal involvement is at a minimum. Also, make sure that the exact day and time of the external audit is a surprise. You and the managers need to always be on top of the system in order to do well.

Things to Check

An external audit should cover everything that's included on each internal audit sheet. However, it can also cover anything else you'd like to keep track of on a periodic basis. For instance, here are some additional points you will want to inspect during an external audit:

- Do the daily sales reports agree with the register tape?

- Do daily sales reports agree with the deposit slips from the bank?

- Is the scoreboard up to date and correct?

- Are all invoices divided into their proper expense categories and filed to be paid?

- Are all checklists being used?

- Is the office clean and organized?

- Are employee folders complete and accurate?

7.6 The Bonus System

Remember that we have created a game with our audits. Now it is time to tell the managers what they get if they win. This is where your bonus system comes into play.

A bonus system gets your key people involved in the mechanics of your coffee house. If what they do impacts your business, it only makes sense to let them in on how it makes money and to reward them accordingly. It develops a sense of ownership towards the coffee house.

No one runs a business as well as someone who owns it. By distributing bonuses to key employees, you are making them players in the game.

Active participants need to know the score (which, thanks to the scoreboard, they see every day). They also need to know what they win or lose. Money talks best. If they can consistently win $200 per month, they can inversely not get that money if the business is losing.

You can really make up any kind of game you want. What I offer here is just one way to do things. You can use it, change it, or discard it. Just stick to some important aspects that we mentioned earlier:

- The rules are clearly known

- The scores are posted

- The game is self-regulated

- The participants can calculate what the bonus will be based on the above

7.6.1 Bonus Calculations

Many small businesses don't have a system for figuring out bonuses. Some give money to key people when they feel the business is profiting and they want to show their gratitude. It may be motivated by some special event, like the holidays or a manager going on vacation. These are fine times to do this, but they hardly fit into the rules of a good game.

With a bonus system, you want to satisfy that most basic need of "What's in it for me?" It really is important for your key people to see that they will somehow benefit from their efforts to run the coffee house well. Also, a bonus is a way for you, the owner, to say to your key people that you know they are doing a good job. We all long for some sort of recognition for a job well done.

There are many ways to calculate a bonus. It could be a straight percent of sales or net profit, for example. However, the problem with doing it this way is that you can have good sales and not make a profit, or you can show a net profit that isn't a true picture of profitability. Some expenses may only pertain to the owner, and a manager has no control over that expense.

So how do you figure out a fair way? I like to make it depend on what the key employee can have some impact on. The way I figure out is to subtract controllable expenses, cost of sales, and labor from the total sales in order to come up with an amount I can take a percentage from.

Total Sales – Cost of Sales – Labor – Controllable Expenses = Bonus Fund

Once you have calculated your bonus fund, you can assign a bonus percentage to each employee. For instance, the assistant manager could get two percent of that fund. A shift manager might get one and a half percent. You can use the percent figure in raises also. Instead of a raise in salary, you can raise the amount of their bonus. That way it is based on their good work. It allows a lot of flexibility in compensation.

Once the manager knows the formula, it becomes real. They can actually calculate it themselves based on real numbers. When you know how to keep score, you play to win!

7.6.2 How the Audit Affects Bonuses

It is one thing to show a profit, but what good is it if it comes at the expense of customer service and repair costs? The purpose of auditing is to make sure everything is running according to our system. You need to give the audit some teeth and bring it into the game. You do this by having it affect the bonuses.

Use the internal and external audit scores as multipliers against the bonus fund. You can customize a system in a number of different ways to suit your own needs. For instance, if the audit score is 90 or above (essentially perfect), that would count as a 100 percent, which means your employee would get 100 percent of the bonus fund. If the score was an 87, and you consider scores of 80 to 89 as 90 percent, then they would get 90 percent of the bonus.

They can actually see how much money they didn't receive because of the audit. You may consider anything below a 70 as a "bonus out of bounds" which would mean that their audit was so poor they receive no bonus. Or, you might say that a 95 or higher on the external audit counts for 110 percent of the bonus.

It's up to you. Make the system your system by customizing it to your business needs or to reflect your personality.

7.7 Building Wealth

Sometimes we get lost in the adventure of building a business and forget that on top of the perks of being our own boss, we can also make money in our venture. However, like all things, success doesn't just happen — you have to create it.

Even when you are making a good net profit each month, if you don't have a system for managing that profit, it can leak out during the course of a year. Then you will have nothing to show for your labor come New Year's Eve. In order to build wealth, you need to know how to squeeze all the value out of each and every dollar through budgeting, saving, and investing.

Through these practices, you can build up a substantial amount of money without having a huge business. That is because time goes by very quickly. Five or 10 years can slip away fast, and if you have a plan to carry you through those years, you will be amply rewarded. The two magic ingredients of time and compound interest are very valuable allies indeed.

7.7.1 Compound Interest and Debt

I like to think of compound interest as a steep hill. People are either on one side of this hill or the other. On one side of the hill, you have compound interest that you pay. On the other side is compound interest that is paid to you. Another way to look at it is that society is divided into two, one half that pays interest, and the other who receives it.

When you first start out in business, you generate a lot of debt. Your $200,000 loan may seem like a deal at 9 percent for 7 years, but is it really? Let's look at it closer. By the time you pay off your $200,000, you will have paid an additional $70,295.16 in interest. That's over 35% of your total loan!

When you are paying off your loan, you are looking up from the bottom of a steep slope towards the debt-free top. Most of the monthly payment is interest — hence the steepness. Looking at the first year on that note, you have paid $21,485.74 in principal (actual borrowed money paid back), and $17,127.98 in interest. That is a lot of interest compared to principal.

By the end of the note, however, this ratio will level off. During the final year of the note, you pay $36,795.48 in principal and only $1,818.30 in interest. At the top of the hill, you are debt-free — you owe no interest and receive no interest.

A business can't really move to the other side of the hill and receive interest, because the government doesn't like businesses to retain profits. You cannot leave the money in the company to earn compound interest. It needs to be spent on capital improvements or dispersed as compensation, triggering taxes. This is where you need a good accountant who can show you ways to minimize taxes while increasing compensation.

7.7.2 Paying Off Debt

Many accountants do not like businesses to pay off debt too fast because it creates phantom income. This is due to the fact that you can only expense interest, not principal.

Let me explain. You never really owned the principal. It wasn't your money; you borrowed it. When you wrote that loan payment check every month, the principal you paid back wasn't yours in the first place, so it is not considered a legitimate expense. Only the interest that you pay on that payment is considered yours, and therefore you are allowed to expense that portion of the payment.

So going back to the example above, you paid $21,485.74 in principal and $17,127.98 in interest during your first year. The interest goes on your P&L statement as an expense, but where does the principal go? Down to the bottom line as profit — profit that you gave back to the lender and that you are taxed on, even though you don't actually have the cash anymore. That is why it is called phantom income. A good accountant can help you deal with this issue, and hopefully still pay the loan off earlier. Let me show you why this is a good idea.

If you pay off your loan in 7 years, you will make payments of $3,217.80 every month over that loan period, which will total $70,296.30 in interest. But if you can swing an extra $1,000 per month, and make payments of $4,217.80, you can pay the loan off in five years and save $21,197.42. That is significant. It also makes the interest hill a little smaller. The key is to generate cash to do this, and to do this you have to learn the value of money.

Here is the best way I can think of to look at the value of money as it relates to your coffee house. It is also a good math lesson to teach your employees. First of all, let's assume that you are netting 8 percent profit before taxes. Every time you spend money on expense items, that is money that normally would go straight to the bottom line in the form of net profit, had you not spent it.

Example 1

Suppose you bought a box of mechanical pencils for $9.95 at the office supply store. How much in the way of sales do you need in order to produce enough profit to pay for them? The easiest way to figure it out is to divide $9.95 by your net profit percentage, which is .08.

$$\$9.95 \div .08 = \$124.37$$

You need to sell an extra $124.37 in coffee to produce enough profit to cover your purchase. Every time you spend a dollar, a corresponding sale needs to take place to pay for the purchase.

Example 2

Cleaning the refrigerator compressor every week extends the life of the unit. A compressor costs $500, so if you didn't clean it regularly and keep it in good working order, you would need to generate $6,250 in sales to pay for a new one.

$$\$500 \div .08 = \$6,250$$

By the way, those sales are on top of your existing sales. You need those sales just to get you back to breakeven where you were before you bought the new compressor.

Thinking about the value of a dollar in these terms can have a drastic effect on the bottom line. If you get into the habit of thinking in terms of related sales to pay for an item, it is a whole different story when you make a purchase.

Save By Setting Up Exclusive Deals

In addition to thinking in this new way, you have on your side economy of scales. In other words, multiply savings by how often you purchase a particular item in a year. We used to buy different specialty coffees from a number of purveyors with an average price of $6.10 per pound. Then, we set up a deal with one specific roaster promoting their coffees exclusively and in return received our own special blend for $5.45 per pound. That is a savings of 65 cents per pound. We typically went through 300 pounds a year, so that was a savings of $195 — the same as an additional $2,437.50 in sales!

I'm sure you can think of plenty of things that you go through a lot, from paper towels to paper coffee cups. If you can save just 5 cents on an item that you purchase thousands of per year, that can translate into the equivalent of thousands of dollars in additional sales that you didn't need.

Forced Savings Account

Now for something radical: set up a forced savings account. In a forced savings account, you automatically transfer a specific amount of money (how large or small is up to you) from your checking account into an interest-bearing account on a certain day of the month. It follows the old rule to "Pay yourself first." If you do not do this, the year will slip by, and you will have nothing to show at the end for your efforts.

Start with something small just to see how it goes. Even $100 a month. This is easy to do for almost any business. What does it mean? It means that at the end of the year you will have $1,200 plus interest to do whatever you like with. Use it to pay for a vacation, employee bo-nus or a new piece of equipment (that you didn't have to borrow, thus saving even more interest). The fact is that you have the cash and therefore have the freedom to choose what to spend it on. Without the forced monthly savings, you would have spent that money during the course of the year and have no idea what you spent it on.

Any bank can set this up for you. You will find that the interest is better if it is invested in treasury securities. Talk to a stockbroker or investment advisor about different options. You want the money to be invested in something safe, but you also want to be able to write checks from it in case of emergency.

The fun part is watching this account grow every month. It doesn't take long before you start to figure ways to increase the amount of money that goes into the account every month. In fact, every penny you save now has a useful place to go. Hopefully, it won't be too hard to justify $2,000 a month into this account or more. Now we are talking real money.

Remember what happens to interest over time and watch what happens in 10 years. Two thousand dollars a month invested in an index fund averaging 10 percent would yield $412,227 in 10 years. Ah, the power of planning.

There is nothing wrong with creating wealth. It is only through profit that you provide capital to grow and pay wages. We are not talking greed here. It is only being responsible for your own financial well-being. As you save and invest, you start to live on the other side of the interest hill, and your money starts earning without you working for it.

It is a beautiful thing to watch. Eventually your money is earning more than you need to cover your monthly living expenses. So guess what? You don't have to work anymore. At least not for a paycheck. Maybe for more altruistic things. After all, there has to be more to following a business system than just good business. If should be financially rewarding as well.

8. Conclusion

It is a Tuesday morning, 30 minutes before opening, and you are getting things ready for another busy day. You've checked the schedule to see who is coming in that afternoon, and your morning crew has already arrived. After setting the lights and the music, you help the Barista arrange the chairs in the dining room, then you bring out the cash drawer for the register. Going through your opening checklist, you look at the entire coffee house to see that everything is set to open the doors, and a group of four businesspeople comes in right away. They are regulars, and you know them by their first names.

After the morning rush, you go into your office to sort out some of the applications you received the day before and decide which candidates you will bring in for a second interview. Then, looking in your GM book, you see that today's sidework is cleaning the refrigerator compressors. You will assign this job to one of your blue employees, knowing that the job will get done, but you'll check anyway.

During the lunch rush, you help at the counter with customers and go through the dining room cleaning and wiping tables, stopping to talk to some regular customers now and then. At the end of lunch, you gather up a couple of customer comment cards that were left on the tables and write quick thank-you notes on your pre-prepared postcards and send them out that day.

After the rush, you ring out the cash register, replacing the morning cash drawer with the next shift's drawer, then go back to the office to do the books from the morning. As soon as you are finished, it is time for the weekly manager meeting, so you gather up your notes and sit down at a corner table with the other managers.

First, you go over their internal audit sheets, then the external audit that was done a few days prior. The external audit sheet shows again that you lost points for the glass on the front door being dirty. You decide to add cleaning the front door twice per day to the barista checklist. Also, there is one customer comment card suggesting that you add homemade lemonade to your beverage list. This isn't a bad idea, and you decide that you should do this but only offer it in the summer. You ask the assistant manager to follow up with a phone call to the customer who gave you the suggestion to thank her.

As soon as the meeting is over, you discuss with the night manager how the day went and give him a heads-up on a new convention that is in town. You let him know it might be a little busy after the convention lets out for the night. Grabbing your coat, you sneak out the back door. You know from experience that if you try to leave out the front door, it will take you twice as long because you'll want to talk to many of the regular customers on the way out.

Once outside, you take a deep breath. There is nothing like the satisfaction of having a night off, knowing that your business is running smoothly in your absence. You can't help but laugh to yourself. This time last year you were an assistant manager in a department store. That seems long ago and far away indeed!

9. Additional Coffee Resources

Websites

- *Virtual Coffee*
  www.virtualcoffee.com

- *International Coffee Organization*
  www.ico.org

- *Smell the Coffee*
  www.smellthecoffee.com

- *Coffee Research Institute*
  www.coffeeresearch.org

- *The Coffee Review*
  www.coffeereview.com

Books

The following books are available for purchase through Amazon.com. You can also try looking for them in your local library.

- *Bar and Restaurant Interior Structures,* by Lorraine Farrelly

- *Cafés & Coffee Shops No.2*, by Martin M. Pegler

- *The E-Myth Revisited: Why Most Small Businesses Don't Work and What to Do About It*, by Michael E. Gerber

- *The Food Service Professionals Guide to Restaurant Design: Designing, Constructing & Renovating a Food Service Establishment,* by Sharon L. Fullen

- *How to Make Your Business Run Without You,* by Susan M. Carter

- *Loopholes of the Rich: How the Rich Legally Make More Money and Pay Less Tax,* by Diane Kennedy

- *Perfect Cup: A Coffee Lover's Guide to Buying, Brewing and Tasting,* by Timothy James Castle

- *Rich Dad, Poor Dad: What the Rich Teach Their Kids About Money—That the Poor and Middle Class Do Not!* by Robert T. Kiyosaki and Sharon L. Lechter

- *The Tea Book: A Guide to Black, Green, Herbal, and Chai Teas,* by Sara Perry and Alison Miksch

- *Why We Buy,* by Paco Underhill

Trade Magazines

Fresh Cup Magazine

Frequency: Monthly
Rate: *U.S.:* 1 year @ $38 per year
            Canada: 1 year @ $45 (U.S. dollars) per year
Address: 537 SE Ash Street, Suite 300
            Portland, Oregon 97214
Phone: (800) 868-5866
Website: **www.freshcup.com**

Tea & Coffee Trade Journal

Frequency: Monthly
Rate: *U.S.:* 1 year @ $49 per year
            Canada: 1 year @ $54 (U.S. dollars) per year
Address: P.O. Box 416
            Congers, NY 10920
Phone: (800) 766-2633
E-mail: info@teaandcoffee.net
Website: **www.teaandcoffee.net**

More Fabulous Guides

Find out how to break into the "fab" job of your dreams with FabJob career guides (print books, CD-ROMs, and e-books).

Increase Your Profits with Catering

Your coffee house customers could hire you to provide catering services for their parties and corporate events. The **FabJob Guide to Become a Caterer or Personal Chef** shows how to:

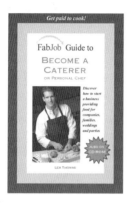

- Set up a professional kitchen and plan menus
- Obtain food service equipment and whether to rent, buy, or use disposables
- Start your own catering business, work with food suppliers, and hire service staff
- Start your own personal chef service supplying meals for busy families
- Market your business, set your prices, and do client consultations.

Get Paid to Plan Events

If the thought of planning a grand opening for your coffee house excites you, why not consider a side business planning events. The **FabJob Guide to Become an Event Planner** shows how to:

- Teach yourself event planning (includes step-by-step advice for planning an event)
- Make your event a success and avoid disasters
- Get a job as an event planner with a corporation, convention center, country club, tourist attraction, resort or other event industry employer
- Start your own event planning business, price your services, and find clients
- Be certified as a professional event planner

Visit www.FabJob.com to order guides today!

Does Someone You Love Deserve a Fab Job?

Giving a FabJob® guide is a fabulous way to show someone you believe in them and support their dreams. Help them break into the career of their dreams with the ...

- FabJob Guide to Become a **Bed and Breakfast Owner**
- FabJob Guide to Become a **Bookstore Owner**
- FabJob Guide to Become a **Butler & Household Manager**
- FabJob Guide to Become a **Children's Book Author**
- FabJob Guide to Getting a Job on a **Cruise Ship**
- FabJob Guide to Become a **Florist**
- FabJob Guide to Become a **Flight Attendant**
- FabJob Guide to Become a **Food Writer**
- FabJob Guide to Become an **Interior Decorator**
- FabJob Guide to Become a **Life Coach**
- FabJob Guide to Become a **Massage Therapist**
- FabJob Guide to Become a **Model**
- FabJob Guide to Become a **Motivational Speaker**
- FabJob Guide to Become a **Personal Shopper**
- FabJob Guide to Become a **Professional Golfer**
- FabJob Guide to Become a **Public Relations Consultant**
- FabJob Guide to Become a **Songwriter**
- FabJob Guide to Become a **Wedding Planner**
- **And dozens more fabulous careers!**

Visit FabJob.com for details and special offers